Think Like Einstein

2 BOOKS IN 1

Think Like Einstein

2 BOOKS IN 1

Peter Hollins

JAICO PUBLISHING HOUSE

Ahmedabad Bangalore Chennai
Delhi Hyderabad Kolkata Mumbai

Published by Jaico Publishing House
A-2 Jash Chambers, 7-A Sir Phirozshah Mehta Road
Fort, Mumbai - 400 001
jaicopub@jaicobooks.com
www.jaicobooks.com

Published in arrangement with
Peter Hollins
1112 Eddy Street Unit C
San Francisco, California 94109, USA

To be sold only in India, Bangladesh, Bhutan,
Pakistan, Nepal, Sri Lanka and the Maldives.

THINK LIKE EINSTEIN
ISBN 978-93-86867-76-6

First Jaico Impression: 2018
Fifth Jaico Impression: 2025

Page design and layout: R. Ajith Kumar, Delhi

Printed by
Trinity Academy For Corporate Training Limited, Mumbai

Contents

Introduction

HERE'S A RIDDLE you may have heard before.

There is a dead man hanging by the neck from a noose attached to the ceiling in the middle of the room. There is nothing in the room, and no way inside or out of the room. There is only a puddle of water beneath the man.

How did the man die?

Unfortunately, I'm going to have to spoil this riddle for you if you aren't already familiar with it: the puddle of water used to be a block of ice, and when it melted, the man slowly hanged to death.

The first time I heard this was in the back of a classroom while we were trying to ignore what our history teacher was telling us about the French Revolution. I heard it in second period at nine in the morning, and I cornered the friend who told me about it during lunch. I continued to pepper him with "yes or no" questions, as the game allowed. After school, I did the same until his mother came to pick him up in her car.

I didn't get too much done the rest of that day, and I didn't get my satisfaction until history class again the next day when I demanded the answer from my friend. After he told me, it seemed so simple and so obvious. Why couldn't I have figured that out on my own?

I didn't know it at the time, but I was making the mistake of thinking too literally. The questions I kept asking were about how someone must have broken into the room and slain the man and snuck back out, and that the room only had the illusion of impenetrability. I couldn't think outside the box and view the puddle of water as something different – a block of ice, as it could have been a few hours ago.

Once my friend told me the answer to the riddle, it felt like my mind had been opened to some degree. Now, I knew to think about individual elements, what they were, and what they could be – not just what they currently were at face value. But in the years since high school, I've learned that while it's an important realization to have, it's only a piece of the huge puzzle of thinking creatively, clearly, and in a way that Einstein himself would say, "*Gut gemacht*" – German for good job.

Realizing how the man could have died from the ice melting changed one of the parameters and would have required a stroke of genius for me to find it. Thankfully, I've compiled a plethora of techniques, research, and data that can help you consistently find genius in whatever you are trying to solve.

Despite all of our schooling, we are never taught how to actually think. We're taught how to pass classes and regurgitate knowledge to pass tests, but when it comes to thinking for ourselves? At best, you might have one creative writing course, and at worst, it's discouraged because teachers must be correct.

There are scientifically proven ways to think better. You might not write a theorem to disprove Einstein's theory of general relativity, but you will make fewer mistakes, make better decisions, and overall be smarter about what you choose to believe. There are ways to consistently think better. You might be left with more questions, but sometimes asking the right questions is far more important because you'll know where to find the answers.

Now, think fast: Janet and Daniel are found dead on a table with only broken glass and water around them. How did they die? I won't spoil this one for you here – the answer is at the end of this book.

– Peter

1

Obstacles to Clarity of Thought

TO MANY people, crystal clear thinking is as easy as being aware of the fact that you might *not* be thinking clearly at the moment.

Do we just need to be G.I. Joe and proclaim that "knowing is half the battle"? Not quite. Unfortunately, it's much more than that.

Thinking clearly and effectively is far harder than we think, even after gaining awareness and knowledge because of the ingrained ways we are programmed to perceive things. We also have many bad habits surrounding our thinking that may have made sense in other contexts or times, but hold very little use in this modern age.

Most of your obstacles to clear thinking are going to come in the form of one of the following:

1. Inertia and Sloth
2. Incorrect Logic
3. Incorrect Perception
4. Rigid Thinking

I'll go through each of these obstacles in more detail so you can see what applies to you and what might not.

Inertia and Sloth

Inertia and sloth is probably the most common obstacle to clear thinking. The reason? It's hard!

Humans innately don't want to work hard or do more work than is necessary to satisfy our goals. Once we meet a goal, the vast majority of us simply shut down. What we want to reserve our energy for, who knows, but we like the path of least resistance precisely because it allows us to make that choice. It also allows us to change and adapt as little as possible in the hopes that we can get through something with a patchwork of thinking and effort.

Humans are lazy and it clearly affects the way we think and act, mostly to our detriment.

If you are going to drive to the supermarket, it might

take ten minutes. You may not buckle your seat belt, you may not use the trunk, so all your belongings will roll around in the back seat. You also may not fill up the gas, thinking your car can survive the ten minute trip without problems. You might also ignore the "CHECK-UP NEEDED" light that has appeared on your dashboard for the past month. Finally, you decide to hold a cup of juice in your hand instead of putting it into a bottle and using the cup holder in the car.

In the grand scheme of things, you might get away of all of this for that ten minute ride to the supermarket for your ice cream. In fact, ninety-nine times out of a hundred, nothing will go wrong, and your sloth will be validated. In fact, because it works ninety-nine out of one hundred times, you might start to believe that it is the best way.

However, that doesn't mean it *is* the best way of doing things. Your patchwork of inertia and sloth starts to break down when you engage in longer car trips. If you were planning on taking a ten-hour road trip, you wouldn't do any of these things – one would hope. You adequately prepare and tune up your car, make sure the gas tank is full, and definitely wear your seat belt. You'd do the preparation to make sure you can make the long trip without a problem, and generally optimize the trip.

That's a big task and you would probably prepare for it as such.

Most of us are stuck in the mode of thinking as if we are going on a simple ten-minute car ride. In other words, we are taking the path of least resistance and only picking the lowest hanging fruit in the hopes it will get us where we need to be. We might solve the immediate problem we are facing, or get through to the next moment, but it definitely isn't the way of clearest or optimal thinking.

If you are eating at a restaurant with friends and want to calculate everyone's share to pay including the tip, you might rely on a tip calculator phone app. What if you forget to bring your phone? You've relied on a shortcut borne of sloth that leaves you unprepared to effectively think about how to calculate a waiter's tip.

If you are playing chess against a novice, you might be able to convince yourself that you're quite clever and skilled by using the same move against everyone to gain checkmate. But this strategy will utterly fail once you start to play higher-ranked players.

Just because you were able to make an immediate problem go away doesn't mean you actually know how to solve it!

Inertia and sloth lead to close-mindedness and stubbornly sticking to your thought patterns, when the only reason you had them in the first place was because you were too lazy to seek a real solution. You are focusing on the immediate moment instead of thinking about the future, and this can be a significant detriment to clear thinking.

It's also completely natural and understandable, so be careful.

Incorrect Logic

The next big obstacle to clear thinking is incorrect logic.

That's a phrase that can mean a lot of things, but I mean something very precise in this context. People use incorrect logic in the sense that they fall prey to logical fallacies on a daily basis. Logical fallacies are errors in thinking that occur because we see an argument and don't necessarily examine it deeply enough to see that the argument isn't actually very convincing. In other words, a logical fallacy is when a reason to do something actually isn't a reason at all under all the flash and glitz. As you might imagine, logical fallacies and incorrect logic are extremely popular with politicians and those seeking to mislead others.

However, they are exceedingly easy to fall prey to and even use. I want to present a few common logical fallacies here to demonstrate just how prevalent they can be in influencing your thinking. In some sense, it's scary that there are so many small holes in commonly parroted logic that leads to flat-out incorrect thinking.

First, there is the ***straw man argument.***

Here's how it sounds:

Argument: "This is why the gym should be closed."

Straw man: "So you're saying you're against health and for the obesity epidemic of this country?"

You: "Well, that wasn't really what I was saying..."

An argument is put forth, and then that argument is refuted by the straw man, which actually isn't even the same argument. The straw man suddenly and subtly changes the argument to health and obesity, where the first argument is only about the gym itself. Therefore, the straw man argument is when a false argument is created, yet treated as the same issue, to be more easily refuted. As you might guess, it's much easier to win an argument against a straw man, in this case, obesity and a nation's health.

They're hard to catch, but people love to use straw man arguments when they feel like they have nothing legitimate on their side, so they have to make their arguments about the implications, or ripple effect, and not the argument itself.

Similarly, this is how people use the same logical fallacy of the slippery slope, which often leads to a straw man argument. The slippery slope argument functions the same way. Instead of addressing the actual argument, the argument turns into the vast variety of implications that one can dream of or imagine. It is so named because a slippery slope is something people happen upon accidentally that can quickly lead to them falling down a cliff of unintended consequences.

Argument: "This is why the gym should be closed."

Slippery slope: "That's a slippery slope, though. Why stop at gyms? What if you want to close hospitals and schools next?"

The slippery slope soon turns one simple issue into everything negative that it may remotely imply or be related to. It's a completely illogical argument to make because it sidesteps the actual topic or issue, but it's one that people use frequently. In fact, you might be the one using it to persuade people to your side, but it's a significant detriment to clear thinking if you don't realize you are doing it. You are blowing something out of proportion, which then makes it an emotional issue. Catch it and nip it in the bud, even if that means weakening your argument or stance.

Second is the ***No True Scotsman*** logical fallacy.

This is a logical fallacy which gives you the ability to refute just about anything but adding the phrase, "But she's/he's not a *real* X!" Whatever the topic is, you are redefining in on your own terms and making it so you are never in the wrong. Most people will never notice this, but they will be annoyed at how you seem to be moving the goalposts.

> Argument: "The study said all sushi in the world has trace amounts of mercury in it."
>
> No True Scotsman: "Yes, but no true fisherman would catch fish like that, not in Japan I bet."

People (or you) may do this if you feel backed into a corner or with no real argument. It depends on people not seeing that you are changing the rules of the game right in front of them just to come out on top. In fact, you are better informed and smarter than the other person because you have specialized knowledge and know the true nature of things better.

It is a logical fallacy because it allows you to slip out of anything with a new definition, despite the fact that definitions are commonly understood and generally set in stone. Again, and this just might be a trend you notice, the actual topic is ignored in favor of something questionably related that you can *win* on.

The No True Scotsman logical fallacy is about changing the parameters to suit you.

The third logical fallacy is confusing where the ***burden of proof*** lies.

> Bob: "I think this restaurant serves fish."
>
> John: "No, it doesn't."

Bob's Incorrect burden of proof: "Oh, yeah? Prove it!"

Does anything seem wrong with the above?

This logical fallacy is a bit sneakier than the others. To most, nothing will seem out of place, but consider who made the first assertion: Bob. Bob then essentially says that he doesn't need to prove John's claim, John must prove that Bob is wrong. Yet, Bob made the assertion that there was fish in the restaurant, so he's actually the one who needs to prove it – not John. Bob makes the mistake of thinking that the person who challenges an assertion must prove themselves.

An assertion is not automatically true. He is assuming it is true, and treating it as a given, or as the truth. Read it again and you can see where the error was made. As I mentioned, this logical fallacy is covert, and that's why most people don't realize they are committing or hearing it. Let's try this with another example.

Bob: "The sky is red."

John: "Are you sure? I think it's blue."

Bob: "Oh yeah? Prove it!"

In this example, it is easier to see that Bob is actually the person who needs to prove themselves, not John. John is only asking a question as to the validity of his statement. It makes no sense to ask someone for the validity of their statement where they are questioning the validity of your statement. In general, whoever speaks first or makes an assertion that confirms or denies the status quo is the person to be questioned. You wouldn't question the questioner about the veracity of their question. Try to keep your eyes peeled for the incorrect logic regarding the burden of proof.

These logical fallacies might not all be new, but it's important to see just how common they are in daily life. All of the examples could plausibly occur to you, and you may notice that something is off, or you may not. More likely you may not notice it every time, so it's important to catch what you can.

Incorrect Perception

Incorrect perception is the third means by which people don't think clearly. This is different from incorrect logic because incorrect logic makes people think 1 + 1 = 3 by accident, though they might know that it's wrong. They've just been tricked.

Incorrect perception, typically known as cognitive bias, makes people think 1 + 1 = 3 and believe it to be true. Incorrect logic lies in the end result, where as incorrect perception lies in the thought process.

The first piece of incorrect perception lies in our tendency to ***measure by contrast***.

It's the error of being swayed by a relative value in comparison to something that doesn't matter versus the absolute value, which is very often the metric you should actually be considering.

Let's say the expensive new car you are looking at has a sticker price of $50,000. The used car is only $10,000. However, the new car is currently discounted from the original price of $90,000.

That sure makes it more attractive, doesn't it? Sometimes we get caught in this trap of perceived value. It sounds like a good deal to get a $90,000 car for almost half off, but that assumes that the car is actually worth $90,000, and that $50,000 is also a fair price. By introducing the comparison to the number that isn't exactly relevant, one might actually feel that they're getting a steal at $50,000.

However, this isn't considering the car on its own merits or its own absolute value. This is considering it only in comparison to something it shouldn't: a relative value which makes it appear attractive.

You are stuck on a fundamental misunderstanding of value, not wanting to miss out on something versus evaluating something in a vacuum by itself. Life doesn't operate in a vacuum, but it's important to keep your focus on the factors that actually matter in your decisions.

In this example, the best course of action would be to judge if the car is actually worth $50,000, despite how much of a discount the price represents. Then you can compare the absolute value of both the new and old cars at their respective price points to make a better decision free of cognitive bias. Otherwise, you just might be fooled into caring about something that is wholly irrelevant to what you are trying to accomplish.

The second cognitive bias that clouds our thinking is known as the ***Gambler's Fallacy***.

The Gambler's Fallacy is essentially the feeling that there are predictable patterns in what are actually random sets of events.

For example, if you roll dice, you might feel that you should eventually roll a seven because it's time for it to happen. Never mind the fact that this is not statistically or probabilistically sound, you are attempting to create order in something impossible to have control over.

This is a cognitive bias that causes us to keep attempting something or hold out for hope when it truly makes zero sense to do so. It's going to cause us to keep missing other alternatives and deciding in a purely illogical manner.

You are also attempting to find logic and an explanation for a random series of events. There is no better illustration than how early mankind started to see entire scenes in the night sky in the form of constellations. The stars in the sky are certainly randomized, but there is the tendency to find patterns, make familiar, and put things into contexts we already know.

The Gambler's Fallacy is overall the notion that just because X happened, Y should happen, X shouldn't happen, or X should happen again. More often than not, they are all independent of each other, and this should guide your decision making to be less biased.

The third cognitive bias that is detrimental to your thinking is the ***tendency to prefer simplicity.***

The first cognitive bias is that humans tend to prefer simplicity. In fact, we trust something is more accurate the simpler it is. By contrast, we also distrust things the more complex they are, or the more hoops we seem to have to jump through. We trust it less and we even become suspicious of it because we feel that decisions should be simple and straightforward.

We prefer simplicity in all walks of life, and that means the path that seems the simplest, or with the least amount of moving parts, is almost always going to be preferred. They feel more trustworthy, like everything is transparent.

This also implies another aspect of what we prefer – we prefer things that we understand easily and immediately. If we can't, then it's as though there is a logical disconnect and something is being hidden. Never mind the fact that many concepts cannot be broken down in such a fashion, but that's why this is a cognitive bias.

Studies have dubbed this *cognitive fluency* – how easily information is digested and understood. If information is easier and more closely resembles a model you already understand and can make a comparison to, it will feel familiar and fluent as a result. For example, there is a science to branding and marketing, and studies have found that easily pronounceable names and recognizable logos perform far better than others. It's the power of simplicity.

We love to quickly be able to ascertain the major points of competing decisions, and if we can't, then we mentally write them off. We can try to push things into that worldview, but it isn't representative of the real world.

Rigid Thinking

The final main obstacle to clarity of thought is rigid thinking, which is when you attempt to view the world through the lens that only your particular set of experiences and social conditioning could have created.

You could also call this close-mindedness and the unwillingness to consider disparate points of view. Whatever the name, these harm your clear thinking because people tend to create a subjective worldview out of wholly objective events. Events themselves are neutral, and are only positive or negative based on the worldview one holds towards them. It's imperative to be able to see both sides and step outside the box of your rigid thinking.

Rigid thinking tends to spring from two primary sources. The first of these sources are stereotypes and what are known as schema.

You are likely able to articulate what a stereotype is. It's when you make an assumption based on your perception and experience with a certain topic, one that generally holds true across your experiences and perceptions. When you have a stereotype about something, you make blanket statements that apply to it in a general sense.

For example, if I said I met someone who loved to knit, had a bad hip, and frequently fell asleep listening to the radio, you might assume that I had met an eighty-year-old. That's because these traits fit our stereotype of someone who is elderly, and we have a broad range of traits and assumptions when we think of the term elderly. Stereotypes contribute to rigid thinking because we have a tendency to immediately classify if something fits our stereotypes or not, and make instant judgments based on that.

Stereotypes present two major problems. First, though stereotypes might apply ninety percent of the time, there is still a ten percent rate of failure. That's an optimistic figure, though, realistically stereotypes are much less accurate than ninety percent. This is clearly a detriment to smart thinking and making the correct judgment.

Second, not all of us have the same stereotype. To some of us, the above stereotype might fit a teenager who just happened to have a bad fall from playing baseball. There is no way of standardizing stereotypes because they are based on personal experience. This means not only do stereotypes cause errors in our own thinking, it might be an error that no one can help you with or relate to because it's based on your personal experiences. They put you into a world of your own that is separate from reality and anyone else's perception.

Closely related to stereotypes are schema – schema are ways we mentally and subconsciously make sense of the world based on our experiences. We form schema because they are like shortcuts for us to use in unfamiliar or new situations. They are more all-encompassing than stereotypes.

For example, a schema might be about how to act in a fancy restaurant, or how to order a drink at a Starbucks. You take a mental snapshot of everything within that context and that snapshot informs your actions within that context for the rest of your life. Sometimes, schema can be very difficult to let go of, which is unfortunate considering they have the same pitfalls as stereotypes: they are never completely accurate because they are meant to quickly inform you about a context, and your schema are likely different from anyone else's.

Because schema are based on people's particular experiences to create a mental shortcut, they aren't necessarily representative of reality. They might even be entirely wrong – like if you saw someone eat with their hands in an expensive, fancy restaurant the first seven times you were there. It might hardcoded in your head and difficult to let go of. It will just feel *right* to eat with your hands, and you will feel odd using utensils for a while after.

Everything in our experience has helped us form, and told us to rely on these stereotypes and schema, so you can imagine how that contributes to rigid thinking, even in the face of a clear rebuttal. In other words, if you have just learned that 1 + 1 = 2, but your experiences, stereotypes, and related schema all told you 1 + 1 = 3, it's going to be very difficult to digest, and you might resort to a logical fallacy or cognitive bias to rationalize not having to change your perspective.

The second aspect of rigid thinking is that our actions are far more dictated by how we are socialized and imprinted upon from youth. Of course, we are all the sum of different experiences, but we are also the result of different cultures, customs, and social conditioning that influence how we think. In fact, they bias how we think and make objectivity difficult to achieve.

If someone born in a communist country debates someone from a capitalist country, each person is influenced by how they were socialized and brought up, and that is effects what they bring to the debate. Even if they try to not let their backgrounds influence them, this level of conditioning and upbringing is subconscious on some level. That's impossible to escape when you inherit and assimilate views and attitudes since childhood. You were born in a particular location, to a certain culture and race, and these significantly color your social conditioning in a way that can make you think sub-optimally, emotionally, or defensively. We all had different third-grade teachers who taught us the same subject in different ways.

In the best of scenarios, social conditioning can you give special insight into someone's perspective and help you uncover someone's unspoken thoughts and motivations. However, most of the time, it will just make you less able to see and understand other people's perspectives, or even the reality right in front of your face.

Indeed, that is the danger with social conditioning and rigid thinking in general. They are so deeply ingrained that they are just how you feel like the world is, and you aren't aware there are different views.

As you can see, there are numerous obstacles to clear thinking, so much so that it might be enough just to avoid these pitfalls to think like Einstein. They might be subconscious and sneaky, but awareness is often the first step to better thinking.

2

Three Frameworks of Thinking

THOUGH CLEAR and critical thinking can take many forms, it's always helpful to look at established frameworks. These frameworks allow us to learn approaches to smart thinking that resonates with us and discard those which do not. They are overall good teaching tools because they strive to be thorough and complete.

In essence, they provide the building blocks on how to think critically and intelligently about any topic that comes your way. After a review of three of the most prevalent models of thinking, you'll be able to see what they all have in common, as well as what they have in common with the scientific method.

Here's a hint: it's a lot more than you would expect.

Especially for a skill as esoteric and abstract as *thinking* can appear to be, frameworks can ground you in real principles. One might be tempted to ask overall what critical thinking is – the definition including adjectives and skills to improve. I'm hesitant to provide one, and instead prefer to point you towards these frameworks, because they will clearly denote skills and sub-skills to help you improve the umbrella term of better critical thinking.

The three models of critical thinking are:

1. The Facione Six Part Model of Critical Thinking
2. The RED Model of Thinking
3. The Paul-Elder Model of Critical Thinking

The Facione Model

The Facione Model was formulated by Professor Peter Facione and lists six skills that contribute to critical thinking. The six skills are:

1. Interpretation
2. Analysis
3. Inference
4. Evaluation
5. Explanation
6. Self-regulation

They do not necessarily need to flow in any sequential order, they are merely different angles to think outside the box and evaluate a situation or decision from all angles. You can imagine that if you neglected all six of these skills, or were stuck emphasizing only one of them, your assessment of a situation would be sorely lacking. The same applies for the other frameworks of thinking.

Interpretation is the ability to understand the information you see and hear and also accurately communicate that information to others. It is the ability to look at something and extract meaning from it that you can use, and also collect data in a detailed and thorough manner. Take the context into account and make sense on both emotional and logical levels.

If you look at a chart, what do you see? Someone with good interpretation skills will be able to understand what is happening and what the chart shows. Someone that takes interpretation for granted will see it but walk away with little to no new knowledge.

Interpretation is also being observant, present, and attuned to what and who you are observing. There is the main message, and there is what you can absorb that is between the lines, subtext, or implied. This is all below surface level that requires maximum attention and focus. You see all the smaller, unspoken details, some of which might be more important than what was explicitly said. Interpretation asks, "*What am I seeing exactly, and am I missing anything?*"

Analysis is the ability to determine meaning from the information you've observed or collected. If you have good analysis skills, you will be able to make connections between unrelated concepts and see how they can work together. It is not entirely dissimilar from the skill of interpretation, but it focuses more on what you do after you collect the information. What are the assumptions and data involved in the assumptions that you can draw?

Looking at a chart through the analytical perspective allows you to go beyond the raw data and think about the implications of the data and what other dominoes will fall as a result. It branches out beyond interpretation, and helps lead you to a definitive conclusion of some sort.

Analysis asks, "*What does this mean to me and why?*"

Inference is the ability to read between the lines and understand what information is missing, and make an educated guess about what it might be. Of course, it is the ability to infer intelligently. When you are proficient at inference, you are able to see the missing elements of information, what you need, and why they might be missing. Like Sherlock Holmes, you try to put all the pieces together into a cohesive narrative based on the small clues you have.

You would be able to find a conclusion via process of elimination and also explore alternative conclusions based on missing data.

Looking at a chart through the inference perspective can put you into skeptic mode. You begin to question if the chart should look like that, what might be missing, and why the results may or may not be skewed. You have already predicted a general outcome based on the data you've seen, and compare it to the actual results in the chart. Inference asks, "*What information is missing and what is it likely to say*?"

Evaluation is the ability to accurately judge something based on a combination of the person's experience, intuition, and data presented. This is likely the most difficult part of the six skills because it necessarily depends on you achieving a certain amount of experience. Without experience, evaluation is destined to be unreliable. A novice skydiver might evaluate a jump to be safe, but a skydiver with experience knows what to look for, and thus can provide a far better evaluation. Evaluation is the skill of accurately knowing what is good or bad in a given field – a good movie from a bad, a good song from a bad, or a good car from a bad – and being able to articulate why.

Looking at a chart through the evaluation perspective will immediately make you think of how reliable the data is. You look into the underlying data collection and study, and your experience in a given field would let you know whether it was thorough, or had holes in the methodology. Who made the study, how credible are they, and are their assumptions correct as well? Evaluation asks, "*Is this information good, valid, and reliable, or do I not trust it?*"

Explanation is the ability to present and break down information in a simple way such that almost anyone can understand it. Often, the more brief and coherent it is, the better someone understands it. It is the skill of being able to do two things: simplify concepts to explain them from a bird's eye view, yet understanding the underlying logic to be able to elaborate as necessary, as well as being able to articulate the reasons behind everything. Explanation is also the ability to recognize the purposes for why specific information is pertinent to different people and adjusting to that level.

Looking at a chart through the explanation perspective makes someone rearrange or reform the chart itself so it can more clearly communicate a narrative. The chart is made to be visually appealing, as well as emphasize the important information. In short, the chart takes on a life of its own. Explanation asks, "*How can I make people understand this in a way that matters to them?*"

Finally, self-regulation is the ability to think about your own thinking. It's to take a step outside your own head and determine if you are comprehending, or thinking about something, effectively.

You are essentially checking in on yourself as if your brain was a child, and your sense of self-regulation was a parent. Are things going well? If they aren't, how can you correct the course to make things go better? Self-regulation requires a certain amount of self-awareness to see that the status quo or current approach isn't working and that another one could perhaps be much better. It also continually asks if you are seeing the big picture or missing important elements.

Looking at a chart through the self-regulation perspective causes the viewer to question if they do indeed understand what it means and what the implications are. They check in with themselves, and if they do not understand it, find a course of action to make sure that they do understand the chart's message – whether that is through understanding the subject matter, charts, or statistics better. Self-regulation asks, "*Do I understand this? If not, what can I do to correct that?*"

The Facione Model is a mouthful, but provides at least six distinct skills that are associated with better critical thinking. The RED Model is a bit simpler, and adds three additional skills.

The RED Model

The RED Model consists of step-by-step process in evaluating and assessing information, situations, and people you come across. The three steps are, in order:

1. Recognize Assumptions
2. Evaluation Information
3. Draw Conclusions

Recognizing assumptions is the first step, and it's all about separating fact from fiction (or assumption, as it were). Fact is objective, while assumptions are unfounded and largely subjective opinion or belief.

Yet, we treat assumptions like fact more frequently than we would prefer to admit. But the simple truth is whenever we listen to the news, or even to our friends, they operate on a plethora of assumptions that necessarily colors what they say. How else can different people come to completely opposite conclusions on the same set of facts and information? It's because they are influenced by their underlying assumptions.

Different people have different assumptions, and there's no way of knowing how yours compare to theirs unless you're a psychic. It's frustrating, but a big part of critical thinking is to think critically – not confirm, not deny, but examine and critique information.

You could even say that practicing skepticism is part

of the backbone of critical thinking. Part of recognizing assumptions is to play the skeptic whenever you hear information and wonder what the purpose and intent of the messenger is. Then, what the purpose and intent of the information itself is. Then, where the purpose and intent could have room for misinterpretation.

Noticing and questioning assumptions helps you understand what you don't know, and how much of your conclusion or data is based on absolutely nothing. When you can spot opinion masquerading as fact, you begin to see gaps in people's logic. It's like watching a movie and then noticing a giant plot hole – why couldn't the robots simply destroy the dinosaurs with bombs? – then you notice that the narrative has been constructed to specifically cover that plot hole.

Not questioning assumptions can lead to catastrophic results. You can interpret information incorrectly, such as assuming that a figure is in pounds versus kilograms and bungling measurements. You can fall into conflict with others if you assume that someone meant 8:00 a.m. while they meant 8:00 p.m. Assumptions, as I mentioned, are individual, personal, and mostly private.

In a sense, they are your own version of the world – but you don't live in a vacuum.

After attempting to recognize your assumptions, the next step in processing information in the RED model is to evaluate arguments.

Evaluating arguments is where you attempt to analyze information as objectively and accurately as possible.

Consider the sources, the motivations, the intents, the purposes, the emotions, and of course the quality of the evidence on both sides. There is far more to evaluate than the actual arguments, because there is an endless list of reasons people can present evidence in different perspectives depending on what their goals are. If you want to persuade someone, you might downplay opposing evidence and maximize the importance of your own evidence. There is typically a reason people are presenting something, so you must take that into account and take almost everything with a grain of salt, and as we saw before, a dose of skepticism. You must also examine your own biases in interpreting the information, as you might have unconscious biases or preferences.

Do you hear only what you want to hear? A common way to deal with this is to take on your position's biggest detriment or downfall, and then essentially argue against yourself through that perspective. Often, when you give more equal mental attention to something, you begin to see its merits and complexities. You can also see how you deal with directly confronting your belief and making light of it. If you start to become emotionally affected in any way, that's a telltale sign you might be allowing emotion to make your arguments for you.

The final step to the RED model of thinking is to draw a conclusion you feel logically and naturally flows from the data you've collected and bias you've shrugged off. It's likely a conclusion that is narrow and specific, and therefore usually a mistake to generalize it or make it apply to more than reasonably possible. Usually when you are able to truly put your assumptions to the side and evaluate information objectively, the conclusion will organically place itself right in front of you.

But let's not get ahead of ourselves.

If you're pleased with the outcome, what could you possibly be overlooking and ignoring to reach a conclusion you aimed for? If you're not pleased with the outcome, is it because you feel like something is missing or because you discovered that you were incorrect at the outset? That's the final piece of self-analysis to conduct when you are drawing a conclusion.

The Paul-Elder Model

The final framework, the Paul-Elder Model, also has three parts.

1. Elements of Thought
2. Universal Intellectual Standards
3. Intellectual Traits

Where the RED Model is a direct step-by-step process with which to evaluate information, the Paul-Elder Model (1997, 2006) is more about the skills and traits people can use to enrich their thinking. It approaches critical thinking and breaks it down into as small concepts as possible so the sum is greater than the whole. You can probably use the Paul-Elder Model as a checklist for your more in depth analysis and decisions, and you'll notice many similarities between this and the prior two frameworks.

Elements of Thought seeks to break "thought" down into discrete parts, such as:

1. All reasoning has a purpose
2. All reasoning is an attempt to figure something out, to settle some question, to solve some problem
3. All reasoning is based on assumptions
4. All reasoning is done from some point of view
5. All reasoning is based on data, information and evidence
6. All reasoning is expressed through, and shaped by, concepts and ideas
7. All reasoning contains inferences or interpretations by which we draw conclusions and give meaning to data
8. All reasoning leads somewhere or has implications and consequences

The intent is to address all of these issues when you are viewing information. Next, Universal Intellectual Standards are objective questions designed to evaluate the information before you and how you perceive it.

Clarity

Could you elaborate?
Could you illustrate what you mean?
Could you give me an example?

Accuracy

How could we check on that?
How could we find out if that is true?
How could we verify or test that?

Precision

Could you be more specific?
Could you give me more details?
Could you be more exact?

Relevance

How does that relate to the problem?
How does that bear on the question?
How does that help us with the issue?

Depth

What factors make this difficult?

What are some of the complexities of this question?
What are some of the difficulties we need to deal with?

Breadth

Do we need to look at this from another perspective?
Do we need to consider another point of view?
Do we need to look at this in other ways?

Logic

Does all of this make sense together?
Does your first paragraph fit in with your last one?
Does what you say follow from the evidence?

Significance

Is this the most important problem to consider?
Is this the central idea to focus on?
Which of these facts are most important?

Fairness

Is my thinking justifiable in context?
Am I taking into account the thinking of others?
Is my purpose fair given the situation?
Am I using my concepts in keeping with educated usage, or am I distorting them to get what I want?

Finally, we come to Intellectual Traits, which are the specific traits that are challenged and cultivated during this process of extreme critical thinking. These include:

- Intellectual Humility
- Intellectual Courage
- Intellectual Empathy
- Intellectual Autonomy
- Intellectual Integrity
- Intellectual Perseverance
- Confidence in Reason
- Fair-mindedness

The Paul-Elder Model provides so many approaches and aspects to consider that it borders on unusable, since it would be hopeless to try to consider everything on a daily basis. You might even say that about all three of the frameworks for thinking in this chapter.

However, what's important is to draw similarities between the frameworks so you can go into the world armed with something that will work.

In order to think better in a critical manner, it's important to realize there are objective methods to approach everything. Asking the right questions is just as important as knowing the answers, evidence and data is not always what it seems, and you need to think like a scientist more than you might think.

In fact, when we look at the scientific method, we find that it doesn't sound so different from an amalgamation of the aforementioned three frameworks.

The scientific method, as a refresher from high school chemistry or biology, is as follows:

1. Question
2. Hypothesis
3. Experiment
4. Analysis
5. Conclusion

In truth, it's just another way of critical thinking. You think something is true, you test it, analyze the results, including any biases or mistakes you noticed, then draw a conclusion as best you can. At best, our thinking methods should resemble that of a careful scientist taking measurements of water. We need to know how the water increased or decreased, the source of the water, what will happen next, and how to make it happen again. Admittedly, it's difficult to approach our everyday lives like this because it can be exhausting, but eventually the hope is for the alarm bells in your head to be sensitive and alert whenever you come across something dubious.

3

Creative Problem Solving

WHEN PEOPLE think about thinking better, typically this is what they mean. They want to understand how to think more creatively and to solve the problems they come across in their life.

They might consider thinking more logically, or less emotionally, but in the end, it's all geared towards solving problems. If the road is blocked, we just want to unblock the road so we can continue along our way. We don't need to extract meaning or lessons from it.

People just want to answer the question, "How can I solve my problems that I haven't been able to crack with as little effort as possible?"

Most creative problem solving isn't really about uncovering something new or learning something. It doesn't require a stroke of genius or sudden epiphany that only few people are capable of. That's a relief.

It's typically about making a connection between unrelated concepts, or suddenly understanding the underlying concepts that make a problem solvable. In other words, most creative problem solving is about looking inwards and kneading the information you currently have like bread dough until it yields something for you.

Problem solving typically means to solve something like a math equation. *Creative* problem solving typically means, for example, to put a filter over the text to discover that it's readable only under certain types of light, but it was in front of you the entire time. Problem solving is deriving an equation, while creative problem solving is putting on 3D glasses during a movie and suddenly seeing things through a different perspective.

With that in mind, the first method of creative problem solving is to simply change the description of the problem.

Often, problem solving is a matter of asking the right question – to elicit the right response, to make people reach into their memory banks, to give a clue as to what's important, or to make people think below the surface. You might even find that you are trying to solve the wrong problem the entire time. If you can begin to consistently ask the right questions, it means you will be on the path to uncovering the right answers.

The question you are currently facing may not be what matters, so it's important to investigate changing the description of the problem.

If you want to buy a car, you might start with the question of the type of car you want to buy. Suppose you keep choosing cars out of your budget. A more apt question would be to ask yourself what your budget is, then choose cars within your budget. If you have other restrictions or requirements, it changes the question again. It can be as simple as that – but it usually isn't.

The more ways you describe and begin to think about a problem, the more angles and approaches you will generate to solve it. If you want to leave a room and the door is locked, you wouldn't keep trying the door. You would start looking at the window, the vents, or even the floor if you fancy a dig. The question began as, "How can I open this door?" and changed to, "How can I leave the room in any manner?"

When the question you ask is too focused and narrow, or simply doesn't do anything for you, the natural solution is to ask another question and redefine the problem. There are two ways you can reframe your problem.

Find the Problem's Essence

First, you can ask what the essence of the problem is, and what you are truly trying to solve. Underneath it all, what matters, and what is the primary purpose? What impact are you trying to change?

For example, if you want to buy a car, is the problem really about buying a car? No – you buy a car to solve the problem of transportation. If you can't afford a decent car in your price range, it might be a better solution to simply purchase a scooter or bicycle with top-of-the-line gear, which would only cost a couple of thousand dollars. The same amount would net you a car which might break down after about ten miles.

As another example, if you want to get into the habit of reading more, do you actually enjoy the act of reading, or is it more about quiet, relaxation time? Or maybe it's even about learning new concepts. If you don't have the time or resources to simply read books more, perhaps you can solve one problem by meditating more, and solve the other problem by reading summaries and reviews of books so you can learn as much as possible without having to read two hundred pages of self-aggrandizing chatter. Believe me, I see the irony in this one.

If you take your blinders off, you can ask yourself the essence of the problem you want to solve. You might find that it is completely unrelated to the problem you are initially facing. You can do this more easily by asking yourself the greatest benefits you receive from solving the problem, and that will usually tell you all you need to know. A car solves the problem of transportation and convenience, while reading solves the problem of relaxation and learning.

The second question you can ask yourself is what similar solutions already exist in unrelated fields. Any problem you're facing, it's highly unlikely that it is the first time it has happened in history. In fact, it is far more likely to be a relatively common problem that many people have faced and overcome in the past. You're never the first to face your problems.

Thus, this question asks you to seek solutions to similar problems in similar or dissimilar fields to see how they might inspire you. Those same approaches or solutions just might apply to your problem.

Similarly, a baseball bat is used in the game of baseball, but can also be used as a hammer, a weapon, something to hold a window open, or as a walking cane. The same object or element can be adapted for different uses due to its inherent properties, and solutions can be adapted for the same due to its inherent insight or complexities.

Above all else, this forces you to think along radically different lines and borrow inspiration from others. After all, why reinvent the wheel when something wheel-shaped is lurking just around the corner? A similar or related solution just might hold the solution for you as well.

When the Orville brothers brainstormed the first

airplanes, the first place they looked was at the wing mechanisms of birds. When horses were conceived of, they were thought to be horseless carriages. If you want to solve the problem of who must decide where to eat dinner every night, you might take inspiration from a system that the state lottery uses.

Everywhere you look, there are probably sources of inspiration. You just need to open your eyes and understand what you are trying to solve.

Commit and Produce

The second method of creative problem solving is to commit to something and do it to completion. The idea here is that motion and exploration of one idea in-depth is better than twiddling your thumbs and delving into ideas in only a shallow manner, which doesn't give you a clear understanding of what will and will not work.

When you commit, you go down the rabbit hole and produce something. Only then can you truly evaluate whether something will work. It's just like running a marathon in that you can't see the finish line from the starting line. It's only when you start running it and perhaps get halfway through that you can accurately predict where the finish line is. Sometimes, you might not be able to see the finish line until right before you cross it. Only through that experience of the actual running will you know how the marathon feels and just how tired you may or may not be. You'll know that chafing becomes an issue for you, and you tend to get dehydrated quicker than most.

The point is that committing to one of the options that are milling around your head will inevitably get you closer to a solution than thinking about your options, even if you end up being wrong. When you walk down a path, you will gain tools, knowledge, and experience to help you understand the problem as a whole and what might be missing from your solution.

This might come a relief to some because it implies that true creativity and originality isn't really the backbone of creative problem solving. Sound surprising?

Instead, when you commit to producing and trying out solutions, there is an emphasis on exploiting what you already know and going through the motions and reality testing it. Often, we think we understand how to arrive at a destination while we're driving, but when we get into the car, we discover that we are clueless when we are actually put to the test. It's the same phenomenon here; we tend to have a poor sense of predicting reality unless we actually go through the motions and experience it ourselves.

When you commit to constant application and production, you give yourself a better chance at stumbling upon a correct answer or seeing the problem from a different angle.

This approach is perhaps best phrased by George-Louis Leclerc de Buffon, who once said, "*Genius is nothing but a great aptitude for patience.*" Indeed, it's an approach that most of history's greatest geniuses espouse. The more prolific you are, the better chance you have at true success, because the best solutions will often build upon fragments of thoughts you used initially.

Thomas Edison held 1,093 patents. He imposed an "idea quota" on himself and his assistants to make sure he kept pushing for world-changing inventions, yet each small idea or patent was in and of itself a huge success because they often became the basis for bigger inventions. Einstein answered the question of how he was different from other people by saying that if you asked an average person to find a needle in a haystack, they would stop when they found a needle. However, he would go through the entire haystack looking for all the possible needles, including ones that weren't mentioned or that may take other forms. It's all in the name of taking as many shots as possible to solve problems.

It can also be as simple as this example: If I want to build a paper airplane, then it wouldn't be helpful to continually study paper and designs. I would need to actually build a few, see how they fly (or not), then tweak my design based on what I found. I would never find the solution of a successful paper airplane unless I build and discover it for myself.

Combine Concepts

The third method of creative problem solving is to actively combine seemingly unrelated concepts, thoughts, and ideas into one Frankenstein idea.

The idea is to synthesize different concepts and ideas and understand how the beneficial parts can apply to your problem, then disregard that which does not apply or work. There are likely existing solutions to parts of your problem, but no one solution that solves everything at once. What might start as an exercise in creativity could lead you to an approach that you never would have thought of otherwise.

If you want to solve the problem of efficient recycling, you might combine the systems of two different countries, keeping the best parts and disregarding the worst. Often, the best solutions are just a synergy of the best available ideas working together independently.

There are a few ways to think about combining different concepts and ideas.

First, you can indeed view it as a pure exercise in creative thinking. The better you get at combining different ideas, the more you will start paying attention to what comprises an idea and how they interact with each other. You can start to classify them in causal terms and how they relate to each other. You can also take two unrelated items and find the similarities between them and come up with the ideal customer that would want a combination of those two items.

Could you have a chair equipped with utensils as part of the armrests? Why or why not? Or, who would want a product that is both a fork and a board game at once? Someone who loves playing with their food and spends a lot of time at the dinner table, possibly. Forcing relationships between unrelated ideas and concepts necessarily makes you look at something from a different angle.

Second, this process of brainstorming can lead you to understand exactly what you are solving for. You will be able to discover what you want to isolate from each idea or concept you are using, and in that way, discover what you actually want. It's a matter of combining semi-solutions and seeing what overlaps and what is missing.

Finally, you can think metaphorically. For our purposes, a metaphor is essentially when you make a comparison between two unrelated concepts or ideas. You can combine ideas in two ways with metaphors, and you stating what they have in common or not.

First, you can play the "except" game, where you compare a problem or solution to an unrelated concept so you can point out the differences. For example, "This problem is just like needing to do laundry, except..." and then do the same with the solution, "This solution is just like washed laundry, except..."

When you play the "except" game, you will literally say the missing elements out loud and it can be effective for seeing things in a new light.

Second, you can play the "because" game, which is where you compare a problem or solution to an unrelated concept and point out the similarities. For example, "This problem is just like needing to do laundry, because..." and then do the same with the solution, "This solution is just like washed laundry, because..."

Here, you will literally say out loud why they are related and similar. Metaphors are effective because you aren't simply combining ideas. You are actually pointing out similarities and differences in a way that can help you extract solutions.

Make Assumptions

The fourth method of creative problem solving is to make assumptions – outlandish assumptions that fundamentally change the parameters of the problem you are working on. This is essentially another way of phrasing creativity – think radically about the assumptions that frame your problem. Think the unthinkable, then continue to play it out so you can see what happens.

The point with this method is to understand that your parameters aren't always set in stone. In fact, they are often subject to change, for better or worse. You might be able to manipulate them yourself, which will make your solution easier and more apparent.

Suppose you want to put a puzzle together, but the puzzle is wrapped in plastic. You might think this puzzle is forever closed to you, and your first instinct might be to buy another puzzle. What if you change the parameters and make the assumption that the plastic is removable and replaceable? How would you act to put the puzzle together in that case?

This fundamentally changes how you approach the puzzle because you wouldn't be thinking about buying a new puzzle, you'd be brainstorming how to remove the plastic wrap gently and replace it. You'd look for scissors, tape, and replacement plastic wrap. This all came about because you were bold enough to make an assumption that challenged something that appeared to be a given.

Making outlandish assumptions that challenge your thinking starts with understanding the assumptions you do have about your problem. Often, the assumptions we have about a problem appear to be fact to us. You might think that the puzzle is simply unavailable, or you might think that someone must arrive at a certain time.

Assume that the facts and rules don't apply and engage in that thought experiment. Is the end result still the same, or do some facts and rules in fact not matter at all, and were just acting as a barrier to your solution?

If that pesky rule, fact, or assumption didn't apply, you'd probably have an easy solution. For example, you could arrive to work late if you didn't have a coworker watching your time card like a hawk. What if you made the assumption that your coworker didn't care? Then you'd have no issue with arriving to work at 11:00 a.m. every day. Your solution suddenly becomes focused on how to make it so that you coworker doesn't care about you, versus waking up earlier and not being late.

Assume that gravity doesn't apply, you can drive as fast as possible, or you can get lunch for free. You'll find that you are painting yourself into a mental corner which necessarily requires a creative solution.

Here's another example of changing the fundamental parameters. You can assume that the answer can be expressed in an entirely different way. If it's a math problem, can it be expressed with words or through a visual diagram? This begs of question of how many different ways you can think of solving something and expressing it. For example, the question of "what is half of twelve" is quite easy to answer along one line. If you take it at face value, you would use the numbers and divide it in two, giving you six. However, how many different ways can you answer that question? Not all of them are numbers-based.

12/2 ½ * 12

1 and 2 TWE LVE VI

Role Play

Role play is a staple of anyone seeking to think creatively and the fifth method I want to cover here.

The reason is that role play makes us literally think like someone else, and hopefully that someone else is drastically different from us. When you play a role as deeply as possible, you start to assume their mode of operating and thought patterns, even if only superficially. That might just be enough to see your problems in a different light, however.

For example, Sherlock Holmes is always a good role to try to inhabit. What does he represent? Extreme attention to detail, deduction, reason, logic, observation, skepticism, precision, and constructing elaborate explanations.

If your problem was that you wanted to work out an interpersonal conflict with a coworker, how might you approach the coworker differently if you took on the role of Sherlock Holmes? What questions would you ask yourself and others to satisfy the Sherlock Holmes inside you?

Now take the same scenario and ask how you might react differently if you took on the role of a psychologist. What are the traits of a psychologist? They are good at listening, reflecting, utterly focused on the other person, and they use statements like, "It sounds to me like..." They also try to get to the root of issues and discover the reasons behind someone's actions, often ignoring the actions themselves.

I will leave it to you to think of additional roles you can play, but notice that the extremely different motivations of each role drastically shapes how you approach problems and solutions. Each role has a different set of priorities and goals, and they might be priorities and goals that you tend to overlook in your daily life.

Creative problem solving is often about looking in the mirror and seeing the answer that is already there, just hidden. We are conditioned to think in peculiar, rigid ways that make us overlook obvious solutions that hide in plain sight. As I mentioned, it's probably a comforting feeling to know that you already have the solution to your problems, you just need to ask the right questions to draw them out and make them visible.

Creativity can't be rushed, and you can't necessarily plan it even with the methods in this chapter. It is literally the exercise of letting your mind wander, so your efforts should be focused on cultivating questions, mindsets, and an environment conducive to that.

4

The Socratic Method

THE SOCRATIC METHOD sounds like it could be an ancient Greek method of losing weight, but instead, it's an ancient Greek method of discourse, teaching, and learning.

When you boil it down, the Socratic Method is when you ask questions upon questions in an effort to dissect an assertion or statement. The person asking the questions might seem like they are on the offensive, but they are asking questions to enrich both parties and discover the underlying assumptions and motivations of the assertion or statement.

This is to benefit both the speaker and the listener, which is why it's commonly used as an educational tool. Law schools are notorious for using the Socratic Method – where a student will essentially have to defend their statement against a professor's questioning. Again, it's not adversarial by nature, it merely capitalizes on the fact that when you force someone to defend themselves or explain their line of thinking, they will often find gaps in their logic if the right questions are asked and emphasized.

As you might have guessed, the Socratic Method derived from Socrates himself, who is best known as being the teacher of the famous philosopher Plato, and also for willingly being executed by drinking poisoned hemlock for having "corrupted the minds of the youth" in Athens.

So what is the Socratic Method, exactly, beyond asking a series of tough questions that makes people see their own weaknesses? You are putting what people say to an incredible stress test. It trains you to question your beliefs, discard your assumptions, and find the implicit hypotheses you are operating on. You are discouraged from taking things at face value, and instead are encouraged and pushed to pick statements and assertions apart so you can find weaknesses and hidden intentions.

The Socratic Method is also a way of shaping beliefs and assertions, because if you are mercilessly questioned and picked apart with Socratic questioning, what remains afterwards will be heavily tested, validated, and rock solid. If there is an error in your thinking, it will be found, corrected, and proofed with a rebuttal. ***If this is still too abstract, just imagine that you are*** *telling someone that the sky is blue.*

This seems like an unquestionable statement that is an easy truth. Obviously the sky is blue. You've known that since you were a child. You go outside and witness it each day. You've told someone that their eyes were as blue as the sky. Now, imagine someone asks how you know.

There are many ways to answer that question, but you decide to say that you know the sky is blue because it reflects the ocean, and that the ocean is blue, even though this is completely erroneous. The questioner asks how you know that color in particular is blue, and how you know it is a reflection of the ocean.

How would you answer this?

This incredibly brief yet effective line of Socratic questioning just revealed that you have no idea why you know the color blue is indeed blue, and why or how the sky reflects (or doesn't) the blue of the planet's oceans.

That, in a nutshell, is the importance of the Socratic Method. A series of innocent and simple questions can unravel what you thought you knew and lead you to understand exactly what you don't know. This is often just as important as knowing what you do know because it uncovers your blind spots and weaknesses. Recall that it was used by teachers on students, so it is designed to allow people to gain knowledge about themselves by asking the right questions. The questions are essentially tests of logic and knowledge so people may discover what they know and what they do not.

I wouldn't suggest doing this on a regular basis to people, at least if they aren't fully prepared for it. The reason is that this can easily be seen as adversarial and obnoxious. This is especially true if people can't answer your questions, and they realize their assertions are mostly assumptions they don't fully understand, and that their lack of understanding is being fully exposed. For example, how might you respond if someone soundly demonstrated to you that you don't understand why the sky is blue as the example above?

If you wanted to learn about it, it would be great. But if you just wanted to have a normal conversation with someone and they started a line of Socratic questioning, that's not typically a pleasurable conversation for the person in the student role, because they are continually on the defensive.

In other words, choose your battles carefully when using the Socratic Method. There are generally six types of Socratic questions, as delineated by R.W. Paul. After just briefly glancing at this list, it should be apparent how continually addressing these types of questions can improve your thinking and lead you to better solutions and assertions.

1. Conceptual clarification questions: what is the

significance and motivation for bringing up this topic, and why was it important enough for them to say? What do they hope to achieve with it?

Suppose we have the same assertion from above, where the sky is blue. Here are some sample questions from each category you could plausibly ask to gain clarity and challenge their thoughts.

- What does it matter to you if the sky is blue?
- What is the significance to you?
- What does that have to do with the rest of the discussion?
- Why would you say that?

2. Probing assumptions: what assumptions are the assertions based on, and is actually supported by evidence? What is opinion and belief, and what is evidence-based fact or proven in some other way?

    - Is your blue my blue?
    - Why do you think the sky is blue?
    - So what leads you to believe the sky is blue?
    - How can you prove that the sky is blue?

3. Probing rationale, reasons, and evidence: how do you know the evidence is trustworthy and valid? What are the conclusions drawn and what

rationale, reasons, and evidence are specifically used in such a way? What might be missing or glazed over?

- What's the evidence for the sky's color and why is it convincing?
- How exactly does the ocean's reflection color the sky?
- What if the study was incorrect or flawed?
- Show me your reasoning.

4. Questioning viewpoints and perspectives: people will almost always present an assertion or argument from a specific bias, so play devil's advocate and remain skeptical about what they have come up with. Ask why opposing viewpoints and perspectives aren't preferred and why they don't work.

    - How else could your evidence be interpreted?
    - Why is that research the best in proving that the sky is blue?
    - Couldn't the same be said about proving the sky is red? Why or why not?
    - Why doesn't the sky color the ocean instead of the other way around?

5. Probing implications and consequences: what are the conclusions and why? What else could it mean

and why was this particular conclusion drawn? What will happen as a consequence and why?

- If the sky is blue, what does that mean about reflections?
- Who is affected by the sky's color?
- If the sky is blue, what does that mean about the ocean?
- What else could your evidence and research prove about the planet?

6. Questions about the question: forcing people to step into your shoes and ponder why you asked the question or why you went down that line of questioning. What did you mean when you said that, and why did you ask about X rather than Y?

    - So why do you think I asked you about your belief in the sky's color?
    - What do you think I wanted to do when I asked you about this?
    - How do you think this knowledge might help you in other topics?
    - How does this apply to every day life and what we were discussing earlier?

At first, it sounds like a broken record, but there is absolutely a method to the madness. Each question may seem similar, but if answered correctly and adequately, will yield completely different questions. In the example of the blue sky, there are twenty-four separate questions – twenty-four separate answers and probes into someone's simple assertion that the sky is blue.

You can almost imagine how someone might lose their nerve and belief in the sky's blueness after not being able to produce evidence or understand the actual physics phenomenon. During this process, it's common for people to simply throw their hands up and proclaim, "You know, that's a great question. I never thought of that."

It's plain to see how you can use the Socratic Method to conduct thought experiments and opine on philosophical abstractions, but how can you use this in your everyday life?

It's easier than you think.

Suppose someone makes the assertion, "Taco Bell is really healthy, actually."

In daily life, the Socratic Method takes the position of curiosity and doubt, but it sounds like the innocent curiosity of a child. You just want clarification!

Therefore, to the assertion of Taco Bell's healthiness, you could ask:

- Oh really? Where did you hear that?
- Interesting! The quadruple cheesy taco too?

- I've read the opposite! What's different about what we heard?
- What parts of the menu?
- Yes, I suppose, but what about McDonald's?
- What makes you say that?
- What nutritional standard are you using?
- What approach to health makes you say that?

Make sure to use the tone of curiosity and surprise, because that's a far more welcome tone than doubt, which will cause instant defensiveness. They will either entrench themselves deeper in their assertion, or realize that they can't answer any of your questions and become defensive. However, as you can see, just taking the tone of curiosity, surprise, and clarification makes the Socratic Method easy to conceptualize in daily life. You are just wondering about the answers to your innocent questions, and who better to ask than the source of the assertion?

If not on someone else, you can also run through the thought exercise of conducting a round of Socratic questioning on yourself. It's useful in performing what I like to call a "sanity check" – to see that your beliefs or assertions are rooted in something real, and not just spur of the moment emotion or rash decision.

5

Making Smarter Decisions

HOW CAN you deal with indecision – the bane of so many people's lives? There must be a smarter, more intelligent way of consistently banishing it from your life.

Analysis paralysis isn't just a fancy, rhyming term. It's a real problem that can hold you back from everything you hold dear in life, from your personal to professional areas. It's when, despite having all the information at your disposal, and maybe even knowing what your gut tells you and what the evidence tells you, you are paralyzed. You can't make a choice because you aren't sure it will be the best, and you want to stall until eventually you either gain absolutely definitive data, or someone else makes the decision for you.

Actually, the second would be ideal, wouldn't it?

That's part of the reason people tend to be indecisive. We feel that we are putting ourselves – our intelligence, creativity, fitness, musical talents, you name it – on the line when we make a decision. For every positive reaction to a decision, there is a negative one, whether real or imagined. We absolutely hate the idea of being looked at in a negative manner, even if we're completely right.

In other words, it doesn't usually come down to decision fatigue or trying to optimize for the best option, although it occasionally can. We're indecisive because we don't want to be judged negatively. It's often a confidence issue as opposed to a pickiness issue.

For instance, let's take the all-too-common scenario of having to decide what restaurant to eat dinner at. Suppose you are with a friend who makes fun of you for your food preferences and is extremely picky, yet insists that you pick so they can feel generous.

You might feel hesitant to choose a place because you feel like you're in a no-win situation. If you choose a place, they won't like it and will ridicule you, and if you don't choose a place, they will be annoyed that you are taking so long.

This in a nutshell illustrates the most common feeling of analysis paralysis. You feel like you can't win, so you stay still in the hopes that you'll do less damage that way. At the very least, it can feel like an exhausting chore.

Listen up, indecisive people and those of you who are struck with analysis paralysis. What follows are some tips for you to pull the trigger more quickly and more intelligently. I know you thought you had to sacrifice one and you couldn't have both, but it's not true.

First, realize that almost every decision is reversible, and you can take them back to some degree. Therefore, it makes far more sense to dip your toe into one option and see what happens, instead of standing at the fork in the road until you collapse. You learn so much more by acting as if you are going to take option B instead of hemming and hawing about both. It's only in the process of option B will you learn more about it and how it feels.

If you are trying to decide between moving to New York or Texas, are you going to gain more information by visiting neither and continuing to debate with yourself, or by visiting one and seeing how you feel about it and gaining relative information?

Second, as we discussed in an earlier chapter, apply strict filters and boundaries to help you make the choice for you. For example, if you are struggling with what restaurant to pick for dinner, you might apply filters of: healthy, inexpensive, within a ten minute drive, and not hamburgers. After you set these boundaries, you might only have one or two choices left over.

If you're left with zero choices, remove one or two filters and work backward until you can make an easy, yet satisfactory, choice. You'll be left with choices that are within your criteria, and at that point, what does it matter? You can choose at random at this point with no loss in happiness or effectiveness, and you've successfully ignored everything that you *don't* care about.

A corollary to setting boundaries is to first decide upon a default action if you can't decide within a set amount of time. Keep it as short as possible, depending on the context and importance. For choosing a restaurant, it might be five minutes. Once the five minutes are up, go to the default you head. This can save time, but the act of choosing the default choice is important because you will have automatically selected something that fits your requirements or desires.

In many instances, the default is what you had in mind the entire time, and where you were probably going to end up regardless of going through the motions and endless debate. You go through the mental exercise of choosing a "default" with the idea that you might end up there anyway.

Third, realize that "perfect" is the enemy of "adequate" or simply "good enough". When you are trying to make a choice, often-indecisive people are paralyzed because they want to squeeze every ounce of potential or joy out of something.

If that sounds familiar, it's because they are on the wrong end of the 80/20 Pareto Principle Rule. The Pareto Principle states that 80% of your enjoyment will come from 20% of the struggle and effort, but to achieve that final 20% of value, you would need to invest 80% of the effort.

In other words, to achieve a decision that would make you 80% happy, you would only have to invest 20% of your effort. However, to find the absolute perfect choice that represents 100% happiness, you would need to put in an additional 80% effort. Does that seem worth it?

In the vast majority of cases, not really.

That's why "perfect" is the enemy of "good enough" – we don't realize we are striving for perfect until we are left paralyzed for thirty minutes on where to eat dinner. Therefore, many of us need to change our entire standard for what we aim for with some decisions. We should be aiming for something that is adequate and that we accept without a problem, rather than something that makes you jump with joy. That's just not possible in most cases, so in addition to spending far too much time being paralyzed, you are probably chasing something that does not exist.

If something checks all your boxes, that's all you need to beat your indecision. When you aim for perfection, you also tend to start running up against the law of diminishing returns, which states that the amount of effort you put into something isn't worth the return you gain anymore. For example, you might spend a hundred dollars on a pair of nice shoes. At that price point, they will be well-constructed, sturdy, and fashionable. What if you were to spend two hundred dollars on a similar pair of shoes? They'd still be well-constructed, sturdy, and fashionable.

This begs the question: were they worth the extra hundred dollars over the cheaper pair? For most people, no. There is a law of diminishing returns where the more expensive shoes don't make a difference in any relevant way. How nice can a pair of shoes get? Unless the more expensive shoes are self-cleaning with automatic lacing, you are spending more for essentially the same return.

You probably aren't shooting for life-changing restaurants every night of the week. In this case, your compulsion to make a perfect choice is wasted energy. Eating is the goal, not choosing a perfect meal. Unless you are making life-impacting choices that you will feel the repercussions of for years, attempting to make a perfect choice is silly. The difference between the "perfect" choice and the "good enough" choice will be negligible, and you might not even feel it, or remember it, the next day. There won't be consequences that make a difference in the long-term, so what is the sense in spending additional time on it?

Finally, comedian Louis C.K. has clever input on this matter: "My rule is that if you have someone or something that gets seventy percent approval, you just do it. 'Cause here's what happens. The fact that other options go away immediately brings your choice to eighty. Because the pain of deciding is over."

Fourth, engage in intentionally judgmental thinking. This is the type of thinking you have probably tried to repress, but it will be very beneficial for your decision-making. Think in black and white terms and reduce your decisions down to one to three main points. Willfully ignore the grey area, and don't rationalize or justify statements by saying, "But…" or "That's not *always* true…"

The idea is to focus on what really moves the needle for you, and ignore things that, while they matter, aren't the most important things. Sometimes, consuming less information will help this because you are focused on a smaller set of factors.

Let's go back to the example of choosing a restaurant for dinner. How can you think more in black and white terms about something like this?

Simply reduce your restaurant choices down to what you might think is a first impression. Restaurant A is a place for burgers, despite the fact that there are five menu items that are not burgers. It doesn't matter – in black and white terms, it's a burger place.

Restaurant B is expensive, despite the fact that it has three items that are pretty cheap. It doesn't matter – in black and white terms, it's expensive.

Restaurant C is far away, despite the fact that if you hit good traffic, it's not too far. It doesn't matter – in black and white terms, it is far.

Seeing options in black and white terms basically generalizes their traits and removes their subtleties. Remember, if we're talking about destroying indecision, this is one of the best things you can do. For your taste buds, that's another matter.

Beating analysis paralysis in general is a matter of understanding why you feel mired amongst choices and not destinations, and taking perspective into account when you think about how much time you are spending deciding, versus how much additional joy you'll receive. Setting boundaries to find essentially equal choices helps, as well as seeing only in black and white.

6

Find Your Intelligence Type

Sometimes, we might feel like we don't necessarily fit into the standards of intelligence or *genius* that are generally accepted.

To be *smart* in the real world can take many forms, but most people have difficulty looking past pure academic and book intelligence – something we might quantify through test scores and an IQ number. Thus, if school is not your strong suit, or you can't be bothered to sit down and listen to a lecture, you might feel that you're inadequate or simply mediocre.

Of course, it's impossible and inaccurate to reduce three dimensional people down to a single number. It's an imperfect way of measuring worth, and this is the chapter to demonstrate exactly that. We are more than simple numbers, and it just requires understanding the types of intelligences and genius that exist beyond traditional academic intelligence.

It was as recent as 1983 that Harvard professor Howard Gardner formulated the specific types of intelligence that people tend to display outside of pure academic intelligence, and he published his thoughts in the book, *Frames of Mind*.

Gardner's overall thesis encompassed how people felt about the limited methods of measuring people's intelligence – they have limited to no relevance to real world ability, capacity, or success. A high IQ score might be correlated with traditional types of success and higher education, but it certainly doesn't cause success in itself.

A world class athlete or musician might not have a high IQ test score, but their particular brand of intelligence and genius has clearly brought them success in other ways. The tasks on an IQ test may certainly measure something, but so does the 100-meter dash. They don't necessarily correlate to genius or intelligence. Indeed, they distinctly encompass two of Gardner's intelligence types.

Based on his research, Gardner eventually formulated eight intelligence types:

1. Linguistic and verbal intelligence – skill with words and language

2. Logical-mathematical intelligence – skill with numbers and logic
3. Visual-spatial intelligence – skill with judging space
4. Body-movement intelligence – skill with body control and coordination
5. Musical intelligence – skill with melody, rhythm, and harmony
6. Interpersonal intelligence – skill with communication and understanding people
7. Intrapersonal intelligence – skill with self-analysis and self-regulation
8. Naturalist intelligence – skill in the outdoors. This intelligence type was added twelve years after Gardner's first book.

With eight distinct intelligence types, you can see which traditional education and schools emphasize – the logical and linguistic/verbal. This is what school tests typically measure, and it's not until we leave most institutional educational settings that we can truly explore or understand that we have different types of intelligence. Some might be tempted to call some of these intelligence types mere skills and abilities, but that's doing them a massive discredit. It's been in many studies that people's brains literally function differently when involved in these different types of activities

(Huang Z et al. 2010. *Verbal memory retrieval engages visual cortex in musicians.*).

I want to delve into each intelligence type to give a brief description. If you've ever felt out of place in a traditional classroom, or that you've been unable to show your talents to the world, it's time to discover your particular brand of genius. People can excel in multiple types of intelligence, and once you understand what you excel at, it is much easier to capitalize on your strengths.

Linguistic and Verbal Intelligence

Some people have a way with words with what you might call the gift of gab. They're never short on words, and they seem to be able to create speeches out of thin air. The same applies with their writing. They know how to engage others, communicate well, and tell good stories.

They know how to express themselves accurately and can help you do the same.

Whatever message is rattling in your brain almost always makes it out clearly and effectively. Communication is the bedrock of human relationships, and as a result of your linguistic and verbal skills, you have many strong friendships.

If you recognize yourself in the description above,

you might possess this intelligence type. Here are some of the specific characteristics.

- You are a talented writer.
- You tell engaging stories.
- You're good with crossword puzzles.
- You like to participate in arguments – and usually win.
- You're considered funny.
- You give clear explanations.
- You have a large vocabulary and easily learn new words.
- You're good with foreign languages.

Logical and Mathematical Intelligence

Cogito ergo sum – I think, therefore I am.

People with strong logical and mathematical intelligence are the people who always got A's in math class, even if they didn't read the textbook. They innately understand the complex relationships and logical flow of numbers and how they interact with each other. They don't have to rely on formulas because the manner of solving a math problem is innate and they can often figure it out themselves.

This translates to other parts of their life.

They can learn more quickly and effectively than others because they can understand logical patterns just from seeing the first few steps. They like the rules and structure that math and logic provide, and the fact that there is only one correct answer. Abstractions and philosophy might be interesting, but less compelling because it is open-ended and functions on hypotheticals and theories. People with this intelligence type are typically high performers because they have figured out what it takes to succeed in school or the workplace, and they consistently complete the formula.

- You enjoy solving mysteries and playing strategy games.
- You are good at logical problems and are constantly on the lookout for rational explanations.
- You're good at math because it just seems to make sense.
- You like thinking about the logic underlying scientific discoveries and theories.
- You wonder how things work.
- You're good with computers and other things that require patience and precision.

Visual Spatial Intelligence

Are you good with navigation, maps, and chess? These are all activities that require strong visualization skills and being able to manipulate things inside your head. Not only that, are you good at reproducing what you see in your head through drawing or painting? You know how far apart things are, how they are likely to react to each other, and what their sizes are likely to be.

If you have ever though you have the skill to be an artist, sculptor, painter, or architect, and you enjoy manipulating shapes and sizes to fit things together, you might have this intelligence type.

- You are good in putting puzzles together.
- You enjoy art and photography – especially the composition.
- You study with charts and pictures.
- You're good with directions, maps, and compasses.
- You can visualize pictures in your head and take particular notice of colors and shapes.
- You tend to doodle or draw.
- You can remember places vividly.

Body Movement Intelligence

Some people were born to move, and you can see by the way they walk or instinctually know how to throw a ball far. They look like they could be professional dancers despite it being the first time they've set foot on a dance floor.

They know how to maximize their body's abilities, and they have an innate understanding of body mechanics and kinesiology. No, they may not ace an anatomy test, but they can tell you what muscles do what and what motions are required to throw a ball far. They understand their bodies well and can manipulate them to generally do what they want.

They learn certain motions faster, and they have superior muscle memory to improve and recall it better. They are well-coordinated, the opposite of clumsy, and generally seem to be good at anything physical they try their hand at.

- You're good at sports.
- You dance well.
- You learn by doing and feeling.
- You gesture and work with your hands.
- You like to build things.
- You're well coordinated and have good motor skills.
- You can't sit still for too long.

Musical Intelligence

How else can you explain the people who have perfect pitch, can sing in tune, and can pick up instruments quickly? Or for that matter, how would you explain people like Mozart, who was writing and performing with symphonies when he was still a young child?

Musical intelligence is both genetic and a product of our environments. Musical ability has been shown to be passed down from parent to child, but it is also best developed and capitalized upon when young. Whatever the case, your baseline level of ability with regard to music, singing, pitch, tone, rhythm, composition are fairly high. You have the foundational skills to produce music, as well as consume it in-depth.

- You have good sense of rhythm.
- Reading music comes easily.
- You learn new instruments quickly, and sometimes by yourself.
- You often sing along to music.
- You can tell a good performance from a bad performance.
- You remember old songs easily.

Interpersonal Intelligence

As you might guess, interpersonal intelligence is when you can strongly relate to other people and understand them. You might even call it emotional intelligence.

You understand people's emotions and feelings without them having to say it. You have a strong sense of empathy and compassion. You're a good listener if you see that the situation suits it. You have the ability to read people and can go below face value to what someone is really trying to convey. You can also communicate well with others.

People who have a strong interpersonal intelligence are often extroverted, love teamwork, team sports, and social butterflies. They feel comfortable among people and enjoy making new connections.

- You can anticipate what others may say.
- You're a good listener.
- You understand what people want and are motivated by.
- You enjoy being around others.
- You have good problem-solving skills.
- You are empathetic.
- You are skilled in verbal and nonverbal communication signals.

Intrapersonal Intelligence

Where interpersonal intelligence is pointed outwards towards other people, intrapersonal intelligence is pointed inwards towards the self. To have intrapersonal intelligence generally means that you think about your own actions and thoughts a lot. You have a high amount of self-awarenes, and with that comes the ability to self-regulate actions and thoughts.

You have an accurate and mostly objective sense of self and ability. You truly know yourself better than anyone else, and you have few, if any, blind spots. If you have ever felt the need to be a psychologist, philosopher, or counselor, you just might have high intrapersonal intelligence because you can detect problems in yourself, so you can also detect problems in other people.

People with this intelligence type don't mind being alone and are comfortable with it. They are straightforward and direct.

- You have deep self-knowledge and you're also self-critical.
- You are aware of your own feelings.
- You have a well-developed sense of self and moral compass.
- You have a strong awareness of your purpose in life.
- You have good intuition.
- You're analytical.
- You prefer to not go with the flow.

Naturalist Intelligence

This is the addition to the first seven intelligence types Gardner deemed suitable to articulate.

Naturalistic intelligence is the ability to feel at home in nature and the outdoors. You innately understand how plant life and animals function, and you can find patterns in how nature behaves. You love spending time outside, whether it be hiking, camping, gardening, taking care of animals, or surfing.

You don't feel quite at home in a city or suburb, and you wouldn't mind living in a rustic log cabin in your retirement. It would give you easy access to the nature you love so much and seek to preserve. Nature is amazing, and you never stop appreciating it. Thus, you might end up as a geologist, marine biologist, farmer, veterinarian, or wine maker.

- You have wide breadth of knowledge about nature.
- You are sensitive to ecology and environmental and animal abuse.
- You see patterns in nature and understand them innately.
- You read about nature and explorers.
- You prefer nature to cities.
- Your favorite activity is to do something outdoors.

What is the significance of these eight intelligence types?

It's important to emphasize that everyone can think like Einstein, just not in the specific domain of his. You might not be interested in, or excel at, logical or linguistic thinking. And that's okay. Your strengths likely lies somewhere else – somewhere Einstein couldn't hold a candle to you in.

What's important is to find what you excel at. You probably enjoy this already, but didn't consider it an intelligence so much as a passion or skill. But a high level of any of these intelligences is what all of the world's top performers possess. You aren't as far behind as you think.

7

Priming the Engine

BEING ABLE to think quickly on your feet and engineer creative solutions isn't solely reduced to what your brain is capable of.

It's also highly related to the condition your brain is in. In other words, let's imagine how an athlete prepares for a big race.

Monica is a runner and it's the night before the national championship. She's going to do her best to not be stressed, and she is going to make sure she gets as much rest as possible. She wants to sleep early and rise late, if possible. She will eat a special meal to ensure she gets the nutrients she needs, and she will drink water every hour, on the hour, to become perfectly hydrated. She meditates for about an hour before sleeping because it clears her mind and pushes the worries and anxieties out of her mind. She needs to prime the engine of her body for optimal performance.

It's almost exactly the same with our brains and mental capacity. They may not be exactly the same factors as how an athlete prepares for a race, but there are far more commonalities than you might expect.

Priming the engine refers to the fact that your brain is your engine, and there are ways of making it run at optimal levels. Ensure that you can think better by taking care of your mental and physical wellbeing in a few specific ways.

Do Nothing

Burn out is a very real risk, especially in today's modern age where to get ahead, it seems that everyone has a full-time job as well as a side career that is aimed toward making money. We seek to intentionally pack our days full of activities, professional and social, as a means of squeezing the last drop of enjoyment out of our lives.

Ironically, this quickly becomes counterproductive because very few people have a battery that can function like that. As for what that means for your brain, any shred of fatigue will affect your clarity of thought. That part should be clear from our own lives. We function better on eight hours of sleep versus three hours of sleep.

However, what's less obvious is that disconnecting from everything and doing nothing at all can actually be a path to greater creativity and insight. There's a reason that when we are zoning out at the gym or in the shower, we seem to have a disproportionate amount of epiphanies.

Thought is inherently fatiguing and taxing on the mind, and is characterized by the brain emitting beta waves. Relaxation and a lack of attention, on the other hand, is characterized by the brain emitting alpha waves.

What are alpha waves also associated with? Studies by Professor Flavio Frohlich, among others, have shown that alpha waves are associated with enhanced memory, creative thinking, and overall increased happiness.

Maybe that's the reason meditation and practicing mindfulness is being pushed so hard these days. They intentionally slow you down and put you into a state of releasing alpha waves, which triggers increased happiness and life satisfaction. Most of the world's top performers, such as CEOs, always mention meditation as a vital part of their daily routine – this is likely why. The ability to tune things out allows them to function at their peak when it matters, like a battery recharge in the middle of the day.

For the high achievers out there, it's not necessarily a matter of taking a break just to generate some alpha waves. Don't think of it as rest, think of it as recovering so you can get ready when you need to really think creatively.

We instinctively know to sleep, stretch, and warm up our bodies if we have an athletic competition, but we disregard doing the same for our minds. When you relax more and do nothing at all, you enter a state of allowing your mind to wander, and you also come back recharged and refreshed.

Allow yourself to daydream because when was the last time your daydreams were boring and routine versus creative and outlandish? If you need a break, resist the urge to pick up your phone and scroll through your social media. Just staring into blank space might be a better use of your time!

Follow Your Rhythm

Your circadian rhythm, to be specific. Your circadian rhythm is the biological cycle that dictates how you adapt to a twenty-four-hour day. It controls when you feel sleepy, when you want to wake up, and when you are at your highest peaks of energy and alertness. There is a particular ebb and flow each day because it's impossible to stay on high alert twenty-four hours a day, so the body has learned to pick and choose when throughout the years. You don't get sleep after lunch because you are digesting; you get sleepy because of your circadian rhythm.

Your circadian rhythm is what jet lag affects, and why you can't simply go to bed extremely early and instantly fall asleep if you want to catch up on your sleep. Why does this matter for better thinking? Think of it this way: you are going to be a much more effective thinker if you can do your toughest work when you are at your best.

Studies have shown that people tend to peak in mental alertness and alacrity at roughly noon and then six p.m. each day, ebbing and flowing between each peak, and finally reaching its nadir at roughly 3:30 a.m. (Taylor & Francis, 2000). Thus, it makes sense to do your tasks that require the greatest amount of creativity, ingenuity, and thought around your daily peaks, and then save your easy tasks for any other time. Take advantage of when your brain is naturally at its best.

However, if you're saying to yourself that you're more of a morning bird or night owl, that might be true, and it is generally a genetic difference between some people (Ptacek, University of California). However, the overall curve of the circadian rhythm remains unchanged in people, whether you are a "lark" or an "owl", you still have similar peaks and valleys of mental alertness. This type of circadian programming also applies to your physical peaks, which happen to coincide roughly with your mental peaks at three to six p.m. (Smolensky, University of Texas, Austin).

Perhaps even Einstein did his best thinking before lunch and before dinner.

Feed Your Body Right

What your mother told you actually has roots in truth. There are foods that you could classify as good for your brain, but they might not be peas, carrots, and vegetables. Feeding your body so it performs to its peak abilities is about giving your brain the nutrients it wants and needs.

Omega-3 fatty acids aren't produced in the body, which means you must consume them. They've been shown to help brain functioning and are biologically beneficial to the neurons that make up our brain cells. Sixty percent of the human brain is fat (Chang CY, 2009), so omega-3 fatty acids can be said to contribute heavily to the structural integrity of the brain. Glucose, what most food is converted to inside the body, is also the brain's primary source of power.

Finally, omega-3 fatty acids contain EPA and DHA, which act as anti-inflammatories in the brain and body. The main sources of this healthy type of fat are either through supplements, or oily fish such as salmon, sardines, or trout.

Perhaps more fundamental and important than omega-3 fatty acids are simply staying as hydrated as possible. If you aren't hydrated, studies have shown reaction times to decrease by up to 14% (University of East London, 2013). When you're thirsty, your brain is literally busy with the thought of water and how to stave off starvation. In other words, a dehydrated brain is using up to 14% of its resources dealing with feeling thirsty, and you can free up those valuable resources simply by staying hydrated.

Water provides the brain electrical energy for all of its functions, such as thought and memory formation. Brain cells require twice as much energy as other cells in the body, so it makes sense that dehydration would affect your thinking efficacy. After all, your brain can't store it, so it needs a constant supply ready for use, and ready to fuel your focus and clarity of thought.

Studies have shown that if you are only 1% dehydrated, you are likely to have up to a 5% decrease in cognitive function. That rate of decrease compounds the more you get dehydrated. If your memory starts getting fuzzy and you have trouble focusing at 2% dehydration, imagine the complications you'll have at 5-10% dehydration. Further studies have shown that prolonged dehydration causes brain cells to shrink in size and mass. This is most common in the elderly, many of whom tend to be chronically dehydrated for years. Water is also essential for delivering nutrients to the brain and for removing toxins. When the brain is fully hydrated, the exchange of nutrients and toxins will be more efficient—thus ensuring better concentration and mental alertness.

In short, make a habit of carrying a water bottle around with you. You don't need to drink sixty four ounces of water daily as some people might suggest, but you could almost certainly stand to benefit from drinking more than you currently do.

The final overarching tip in eating healthy is to eat to reduce inflammation in your brain. I mentioned this earlier, but inflammation in your brain occurs when special brain cells called microglia are activated (Elmore, 2014). Inflammation in the brain causes neurons to fire more slowly, slowing down mental acuity, recall, and reflexes. Sluggish neurons also shut down the production of energy in the cells. This means that cells fatigue easily, and you may lose your ability to focus for long periods of time.

Unfortunately, there are a whole host of things that tend to activate the microglia and, one of the primary ones being sugar, diary, and gluten. However, there are foods that are naturally anti-inflammatory, such as ginger, green vegetables, and turmeric.

De-stress

Finally, keeping your levels of stress and anxiety low aren't just going to make you a happier person in general, they are going to keep you thinking clearly.

The body releases a hormone called cortisol as a reaction to stress, anxiety, and fear. Cortisol will raise your blood pressure and keep you tense, because your body senses that there is a threat that might cause you bodily harm. However, cortisol has also been shown to kill brain cells and cause premature brain aging (Daniela Kaufer, 2014). You also produce fewer brain cells, so stress has the ability to literally shrink your brain. Your existing brain cells for learning and memory function much worse under stress and anxiety.

Finally, chronic stress reduces levels of two critical neurotransmitters: serotonin and dopamine. You might recognize these because they are typically what recreational drugs target because they are tied to pleasure and ecstasy. What happens when you run low on these neurotransmitters? Your brain starts to resemble that of someone with depression (Tafet, 2001).

Manage your stress; manage your brainpower. Diet, exercise, adequate sleep, hydration, and meditation have all been tied to lower stress. Ultimately, stress has power over us because it makes us lose perspective on our lives. It makes us forget the positives we have in our lives, and focus on the small negatives. It's the classic case of not being able to see the forest through the trees. Most of the time, if we stop for a moment and think logically about our stressors, we might find that will be forgotten within the day, and as such, essentially of our own creation.

Slumber

I wanted to end this chapter on another seemingly obvious precursor to better thinking, though it's so obvious it causes everyone to overlook it.

Adequate sleep is one of the most important building blocks of thinking like Einstein on a daily basis. Just as we can harken back to the example of the athlete preparing for a race, sleep is that important for optimal brain functioning. Sleep deprivation will affect everything from cognition, to memory, to speed of thought (Killgore, 2010).

Another researcher, Michael Thorpy, commented that "Sleep deprivation will definitely affect one's ability to multitask. Driving is the most intensive multitasking activity we do—it uses hands, feet, vision, awareness of what's going on. When you're sleep-deprived, it strongly affects your ability to multitask. That's why we have so many accidents with cars, and of course trains. Sleep deprivation drains your executive function."

Sleep deprivation has also been shown to have a negative impact on cognitive functions like attention and working memory. Another similar study found that just two hours of sleep deprivation per night resulted in research subjects performing substantially worse on memory and attention-related tasks.

Sleep specifically has wide-ranging effects on memory, which were first reported all the back in 1924. It's not a new discovery. Other studies have shown that getting a full eight hours of sleep after learning a new task can boost recall the next day. Even a one-hour nap has been shown to improve performance in memory-related tasks.

Activity in the hippocampus increases when people enter deep sleep, and this activity is believed to be the brain's method of transferring memory from temporary "working memory" to long-term storage in the neocortex.

Overall, your mother probably scores pretty well with what she nagged you to do when you were younger. Eat *brain* foods, sleep early, and relax to de-stress and do nothing occasionally. All of these are highly important components of setting yourself up for mental success. Remember, a 1% drop in hydration can result in a 5% drop in cognitive abilities. Every little bit counts, especially if you're trying to make a creative breakthrough.

8

Memorize More

IMPROVING YOUR memory is one of the biggest steps you can take towards thinking better and more clearly.

The term "improving your memory" by itself is actually hazy because we have different types of memory. What most people intend to do is improve their long-term memory, but it's not always what happens. It's helpful to begin any discussion about memory talking about its components so you can understand how to better achieve your memory goals.

There are three types of memory and they have very different purposes.

1. Sensory memory
2. Short term/working memory
3. Long-term memory

Sensory memory holds both conscious and subconscious information you gain from your five senses. It helps you make sense of your environment and shapes your perception. However, you only remember or perceive these things for as long as they are necessary or useful, and that can be only a few seconds. These are mostly things we don't really notice consciously.

Short term, or working memory, is information you consciously remember for short periods of time without rehearsing or actively trying to commit them to memory. For most people, studies have shown this is roughly seven items for up to thirty seconds. In other words, short term memory can hold seven items, but you will likely forget most of them after thirty seconds.

Imagine that you are trying to remember someone's phone number so you can dial it before it leaves your brain. You are relying on your short term memory to hold those numbers, and you can't hold them forever, so you need to rush to dial the number as quickly as possible. The same feeling occurs when we try to remember license plate numbers and shopping lists.

We instinctively repeat and rehearse the items to ourselves to try to push them into the final phase of memory: long-term memory.

Long-term memory is typically the end goal for whatever we try to memorize or learn. Long-term memory is essentially unlimited and forever, subject to how important the information is and how much it was rehearsed.

There are three steps that push information into memory: encoding, storage, and retrieval.

Encoding is when information is consumed and the brain links the new information to something familiar to make it meaningful and make it stay. Storage is when memories are retained, typically by practice or rehearsal of some sort. Retrieval is when you pluck the memory out of your memory banks and access it to use it in some way.

Short-term memory and long-term memory are stored in different parts of the brain. Short-term memory resides in the frontal lobe of the cerebral cortex, but information stored in long-term memory is first held in the hippocampus, then transferred to the cerebral cortex for permanent storage.

These are important because most of the reasons we forget are related to one of these steps of memory creation. For example, forgetting something in your short-term memory is a result of insufficient encoding, while forgetting something from your long-term memory is a result of faulty retrieval. This has been dubbed the forgetting curve by scientist Hermann Ebbinghaus.

Ebbinghaus posited that memories will fade or not

be retained if there is insufficient rehearsal and practice. He estimated that people typically remember only 50% of newly learned information three weeks after exposure, and they remember only 10% eight weeks after exposure. Additional studies have confirmed that it's possible to retain up to 80% of newly learned information if you review and rehearse it within twenty-four hours after exposure.

Our brains are always trying to make sense of the world through limited means. Our memory is selective and wants to filter out the useless chatter we experience on a daily basis. If you rehearse something and repeatedly expose yourself to it soon thereafter, it's a signal to your brain that this information shouldn't be filtered, and actually deserves some mental bandwidth.

In other words, if you learn something on Wednesday, the first time you should review it is later that night, and then every day after. Use it or lose it.

This is the basis for the technique generally accepted as most powerful and effective in increasing your memory: spaced repetition.

Spaced Repetition

Spaced repetition is just what it sounds like.

In order to commit more to memory and retain information better, space out your rehearsal and exposure to it over as long a period as possible. In other words, you will remember something far better if you study for one hour a day, versus twenty hours in one weekend. This goes for just about everything you could possibly learn. Additional research has shown that seeing something twenty times in one day is far less effective than seeing something ten times over the course of seven days.

Spaced repetition makes more sense if you imagine your brain as a muscle. Muscles can't be exercised all the time, and then put back to work with little to no recovery. Your brain needs time to make connections between concepts, create muscle memory, and generally become familiar with something. Sleep has been shown to be where neural connections are made, and it's not just mental. Synaptic connections are made in your brain and dendrites are stimulated.

Here's a look at what a schedule focused on spaced repetition might look like.

Monday at 10:00 AM – learn initial facts about Spanish history. You accumulate five pages of notes.

Monday at 8:00 PM – review notes about Spanish history, but don't just review passively. Make sure to try to recall the information from your own memory. Recalling is a much better way to processing information than simply re-reading and reviewing. This might only take twenty minutes.

Tuesday at 10:00 AM – try to recall the information without looking at your notes much. After you first try to actively recall as much as possible, go back through your notes to see what you missed and make note of what you need to pay closer attention to. This will probably take only fifteen minutes.

Tuesday at 8:00 PM – review notes. This will take ten minutes.

Wednesday at 4:00 PM – try to independently recall the information again, and only look at your notes once you are done to see what else you have missed. This will take only ten minutes. Make sure not to skip any steps.

Thursday at 6:00 PM – review notes. This will take ten minutes.

Friday at 10:00 AM – active recall session. This will take ten minutes.

Looking at this schedule, note that you are only studying an additional 75 minutes throughout the week, but you've managed to go through the entire lesson a whopping six additional times. Not only that, you've likely committed most of it to memory because you are using active recall instead of passively reviewing your notes. You're ready for a test the next Monday. Actually, you're ready for a test by Friday afternoon. Spaced repetition gives your brain time to process concepts and make it's own connections and leaps because of the repetition.

Think about what happens when you have repeated exposure to a concept. The first couple of exposures you may not see anything new. As you get more familiar with it and stop going through the motions, you begin to examine it on a deeper level and think about the context surrounding it. You begin to relate it to other concepts or information, and you generally make sense of it below surface level.

All of this, of course, is designed to push information from your short-term memory into your long-term memory. That's why cramming, or studying at the last minute, isn't an effective means of learning. Very little tends to make it into long-term memory because of the lack of repetition and deeper analysis.

Just as an illustration of the applicability of spaced repetition, Paul Pimsleur discovered that for his audio-based language learning program, there were very specific pauses that led to increased learning. In other words, there were very specific intervals of time between the repetitions that showed better language learning and retention.

The intervals he discovered were: 5 seconds, 25 seconds, 2 minutes, 10 minutes, 1 hour, 5 hours, 1 day, 5 days, 25 days, 4 months, and 2 years. This shows the importance of repetition, especially soon after initial exposure.

Memories are much better created when they are processed and analyzed on a deeper level, because they form a vivid mental image versus a set of facts and descriptions that the brain filters as boring and useless.

Flashcards

Flashcards are one of the best ways to memorize information. They force recall, and they aren't passive. You must actively recall and state what is on the other side of the flashcard, and it's this act of accessing a potential memory that cements its status.

In order to make best use of your flashcards, commit to making two sets. The first set will contain mere definitions and single concepts. One word prompts for one word or sentence answers.

The second set of flashcards will contain as much information about a single concept as possible, so you will be forced to recall all of that with the prompt of a single word. This is also known as chunking information, where it's advantageous to your short-term memory (which can only hold on average seven items) to remember information as a large chunk, rather than as smaller, individual components. This means when you put more information on each flashcard, that set of information becomes one item versus five items.

When you go through your flashcards, put the cards you got wrong back into the middle or front of your stack so you will see them sooner and more frequently. This helps you work through your mistakes and commit them to memory more quickly.

Overall, you are familiar with flashcards and have likely used them, so there isn't much for me to add here that would teach you something new. Just make sure to understand flashcards aren't a passive activity. You need to actively recall the other side of the flashcard, recite it out loud, then strive to recall more from that single prompt.

Mnemonics

A mnemonic device is most commonly seen as an acronym, where the first letter might represent a word for each. You can make mnemonics for just about anything.

For example, the colors of the rainbow are far more easily remembered as ROY G BIV (red, orange, yellow, green, blue, indigo, violet).

Not much more clarification is necessary here, other than to note that while acronyms are the most common, you can create phrases as mnemonics as well. The point is to give meaning to something that you can more easily remember, and this can be different for everyone. Here are a couple more examples: The classification system for organisms is far more easily remembered as Devoted (or some other D-word) King

Philip Came Over For Good Soup (**domain, kingdom, phylum, class, order, family, genus, species**).

The order of the planets of our solar system: My Very Easy Method: Just Say Understand Now (Mercury, Venus, Earth, Mars, Jupiter, Saturn, Uranus, Neptune).

The list goes on. The more vivid and outlandish the acronym or imagery, the better and easier to remember.

Stories

Creating stories, or using metaphors and analogies function on the same principle as mnemonics. They substitute a series of information that is difficult to remember with something simpler to remember that has personal meaning to you.

Here's a simple example of something that I've remembered for the past twelve years because of how it illustrated information so perfectly in my mind. Humans have two types of receptors in their eyes, rods and cones. One is for perceiving black and white, and the other is for perceiving color. Which is which?

Well, traffic cones are bright orange, while rods resemble the silver poles that hold up stop signs. Therefore, cones perceive color, and rods perceive black and white.

What you're doing is drawing out the main

elements of something and putting it into something you understand and remember. Put it into a context that is so obvious to you that all you have to do is be prompted.

Find something with one or two striking characteristics, and think about how it can relate to Spanish history and say, "It's similar to the Inquisition because..." If a story has a good guy and a bad guy, you can characterize them as the historical figures. You can think about them in terms of the difference between motorcycles and cars. A particular aspect might seem like the process of baking a cake. The end result may remind someone of how your mother treated you when you refused to come home for Christmas that one year.

It's much easier to remember a story about a frog who went to the bank than the dry facts and statistics regarding frog populations. A picture of a tree might remind you of the geography of a country because of the curves of the branches.

You can use players on your favorite baseball team to memorize the members of a country's government. Who resembles whom and why? You can use a song to remind you of a history lesson because the song is about rebuilding.

It's also this active analysis and application of a story, imagery, or metaphor to your information that further helps memory become solidified. You're searching to tie new information into existing information in an engaging manner. You might even remember the thought process more than the story or metaphor itself.

Use Your Senses

What happens if you were to discover and smell an old bottle of perfume or cologne that a past significant other used? If you came across a restaurant that smelled like your grandmother's house when she cooked? What does smelling fresh laundry make you think of?

Any of these smells are likely to create a flood of memories to come rushing back. Why does this happen?

The sense of smell is highly tied to memories – in fact, each of your five senses can contribute to memory formation (Fields, 2012). Exposure to sight, taste, hearing, touch, and smell can all serve as triggers for memories, and the more senses you can involve in creating a particular memory, the more deeply it will be embedded into your memory.

This is why hearing a certain song, or how a table feels can take you to a very specific point in time.

Let's momentarily think of a particular memory as a five-piece jigsaw puzzle. If you see something that reminds you of it, you still only have one part of the puzzle – you might not be able to decipher or recall it. But if you see something and also smell something that reminds you of the memory, you are going to have a much better chance of recall. Of course, this means if you can have a memory that involves all five of your senses, all five pieces of the jigsaw puzzle will be present and it's likely you will recall it easily.

In other words, to memorize more, always try to involve as many senses as possible. This might not always be practical, but you can typically involve at least two senses. Instead of reading something to yourself, read it out loud and try to memorize the texture of book's cover. Instead of listening to something, write it down so you can process it visually and light a scented candle so you can latch your sense of smell to something. You are creating more triggers for your memory recall at a later point in time.

Smell in particular is more powerful in triggering memories because its positioning in the brain is physically closest to the hippocampus, where memories are processed. Spanish psychologist Silvia Alava found that people remember 35% of what they smell versus 5% of what they see. That's why we are drawn into bouts of nostalgia and past events when we encounter certain smells. The smell associations are so strong that they often also evoke memories of emotions, not mere events.

Memorizing more not only makes your life easier, it makes it so you can draw on your wealth of knowledge at a moment's notice instead of always having something on the tip of your tongue.

9

The Mozart Effect, Chess, and Brain Training

I WANTED to devote some time to some of the world's biggest myths and misconceptions regarding the ability to think better and boost your cognitive abilities.

Because so many people want to increase the brain's functionality and effectiveness with as little time and effort as possible, entire industries have been created to cater to these desires. But, as you'll read, many of the promises you've heard or read about fall apart under closer scrutiny, and ultimately resemble what you might hear on a diet pill infomercial.

The health and fitness industry is a perfect parallel because people are constantly trying to find revolutionary ways to lose the most weight while simultaneously doing the least amount of work. We usually know the actual path we need to take, but it's typically the path of most resistance and challenge. Perhaps this chapter will just serve as a reminder that there are no shortcuts when it comes to thinking better.

The Mozart Effect

Undoubtedly, one of the most prevalent beliefs is in the Mozart Effect – when mental performance and cognition is said to increase during a period when you have a piece by the famous composer Wolfgang Amadeus Mozart playing in the background.

It's a thrilling proposition that just by introducing an outside stimulus, you can literally increase your brainpower, even if it's just for that period of time. It would be like taking a pill that makes you smart and allows you to exceed your normal capabilities. That's why, despite the dubious veracity of the overall findings in the field, people have taken to it strongly and it has become a billion dollar industry.

The Mozart Effect originated in a 1993 study by Frances Rauscher and colleagues at the University of California, Irvine. The study split participants into three groups and gave them a spatial IQ test beforehand to determine their baseline scores. One group heard ten minutes of Mozart, the second group heard ten minutes of white noise, and the third group heard ten minutes of absolute silence. Shockingly, the group who heard Mozart for ten minutes performed nine points better on the same spatial IQ test, which was an enormous effect. However, the effects were temporary and only lasted for roughly the length of the exposure to the music.

Subsequent studies have been aimed at reproducing the results Rauscher achieved, but with extremely mixed results. In the vast majority of cases, no improvements in cognitive abilities were ever reported. In fact, some studies reported that listening to Mozart before or during cognitive tasks caused a *dip* in performance. Despite the dubious claims, there have even been laws enacted to require Mozart or similar classical music to play in daycare centers and nurseries.

Various researchers proposed many theories as to why there was an improvement, ranging from the music essentially putting people's brains into a state of arousal for better thinking, to the music mimicking the natural rhythm of a certain set of brain waves called trions.

However, nothing has ever been verified because the results have never been consistently reproducible. The initial study by Rauscher actually only had a very specific proposition – that listening to Mozart, or any classical music, immediately prior to a spatial IQ test tends to improve the performance for a short period of time.

From the casual bystander's perspective, it makes no sense that Mozart might improve cognitive faculties unless you were trying to make a classist statement. Playing music would probably only serve to distract someone, especially if they enjoyed the music, and if the music was played loudly. Indeed, some studies also found this to be true.

The Mozart Effect in itself might be completely bunk, but it did give rise to an interesting area of study which has yielded reproducible results. Research has suggested two auditory cues that have actually been shown to increase your brain's functioning.

First, in a 2013 study by German scientists from the University Medical Center-Hamburg Eppendorf, it was found that softly playing *white noise*, the "sh" sound that your television makes when it is full of static, can improve your memory recall. Surprisingly, it was found that white noise affected the brain in the manner that dopamine, a neurotransmitter for pleasure, does. White noise may just block out distractions effectively.

Second, music that can play in the background, and is essentially more similar to white noise, has been shown to improve concentration (Anderson, 2010). Music that is constant, slightly boring, repetitive, and played softly allows the blockage of distracting ambient noise. Perhaps it just effectively blocks out one of our five senses so we can only receive distraction and stimuli through the other four, or perhaps it's the fact that music does indeed cause the release of dopamine, which relaxes people and decreases anxiety, which inherently makes it impossible to concentrate because you are in a state of mental fight-or-flight (Salimpoor, 2010).

Whatever the case, at this point it's clear that Mozart, Beethoven, and even Bach won't help you learn or think better. They might even sabotage you, so be mindful of what you play through your speakers, if anything.

Chess

Chess has long been hailed as a stepping stone to a greater intellect, likely because of its association as a game played by the rich and powerful. It's seen as a noble pursuit, and much more than a simple board game because it tests strategy and thought. Many parents still have the tendency to force their children to play chess in the belief that it positions them well for later life.

This might be true in the sense that they are learning a new game that involves strategic and critical thinking, but there is very little data across a huge amount of studies to indicate that chess by itself will actually increase someone's cognitive abilities. In fact, there are a handful of studies that report an increase of IQ after beginning to play chess, but the vast majority report no change at all.

However, playing chess does contribute to the growth of *individual skills*, so it cannot be said to be without value. If one is dedicated to applying and transferring those skills to other areas of life, then you might see marked improvements due to chess, but in a vacuum, chess is a fun game that simply requires a lot of thought.

To become adequate at chess, you will likely improve your:

a. Memory and recall skills

b. Pattern-recognition skills

c. Concentration and focus skills

d. Problem solving skills

e. Planning and foresight skills

f. Critical thinking and analysis skills

g. Prediction skills

h. Emotional intelligence and people reading skills

These are valuable skills, and the practice of these skills will make you a far more effective thinker. If you take the extra step of applying these principles to your real life decisions, analysis, and thinking, then you might indeed become more effective. However, it would be inaccurate to proclaim that chess actually makes you smarter. If you become great at chess, you become great at chess; not thinking.

Take the example of a soccer player who improves his skills of passing, shooting, juggling, and running. He will be a far more effective soccer player in general if he can transfer these skills into actual matches, but simply developed and maximizing skills doesn't make him more gifted athletically. He will, however, be a far better soccer player than he was, but he won't be able to rise above the level of his natural talent. Chess won't improve your innate smartness, but it has the real possibility of making you think more effectively in whatever you choose to do because of the skills you cultivate as a byproduct.

Christopher McGovern, chairman of the UK's Campaign for Real Education, put it succinctly, "Chess may develop and nourish innate intelligence but will not bestow ability. Chess doesn't make you smarter, but it puts you in a better position for success. The greatest chess players in the world might be bona fide geniuses, but for the rest of us, we might just become great at seeing chess patterns or memorizing combinations." You might find yourself naturally analyzing and planning ahead in your daily life purely out of habit, and that's the real benefit of chess."

Brain Training

Just like passively listening to Mozart to increase your brain's performance seems like a great proposition, conceptualizing your brain as a set of abs to be trained and strengthened is a wonderful thought.

Not only does it give us hope, it lets us feel like we can rise wherever we currently are. We can all become geniuses if we work hard enough, just like we can all have abs if we diet correctly. This is a belief that so desperately wants to be true that people will cling to whatever appears to offer any hint of mental improvement, just like Mozart and the notion that chess makes you more intelligent. We all want to get smarter and think better because we believe our lives will drastically improve as a result. We will become better with other people, we will do better in our careers, make more money, and be happier overall.

It's no surprise when in 2008, psychologist Susanne Jaeggi came out with a groundbreaking study that showed that working with memory and brain training programs definitely increased intelligence as measured by IQ, and that people could boost their IQ by a full point per hour of training. Of course, there were upper limits, but the initial results would potentially be life-changing for people. The study caught on like fire, and indirectly led to the creation of companies such as Cogmed and Lumosity, which sold brain training programs that had impressive claims, such as improving memory to preventing the onset of Alzheimer's disease.

Another landmark study appeared in 2014, courtesy of Professor Adam Gazzaley of the University of California, San Francisco, which touted the benefits of a brain training videogame called "Neuroracer." It was supposed to help adults retain mental faculties, especially as they got older. Indeed, after practice, the subjects in the study improved to the level of a twenty-year-old in terms of game performance.

However, despite the fact that the subjects showed huge improvements, what did it mean for real-world tasks? Is it similar to chess, where you might become better at individual skills, but have no meaning for actual mental ability and capacity? The consistent findings from research in this field showed that when people practice a task, they get better at that task alone. The supposed mental benefit rarely transfer to anything else, so it's a vast stretch to say that brain training games do anything other than make you more adept at "Neuroracer", or matching dots with other dots as you do in Lumosity.

By the way, both Cogmed and Lumosity have been hit with multiple lawsuits for false advertising and claims, and recently Lumosity was ordered to pay a whopping fifty-million-dollar fine for harming consumers, which the company has been unable to pay.

Counterintuitively, physical exercise has been proven to be beneficial for the improved cognitive functioning. University of Illinois psychologist Arthur Kramer noted that aerobic exercises expands the volume of the hippocampus and the prefrontal cortex – areas where higher-level thinking and memory are processed. Aerobic exercise causes biochemical and hormone-related changes that literally increase the size of your brain. For all the complexities we want to ascribe to improving our brains, we sometimes overlook the most obvious answer that is in front of our faces.

10

Deciphering Data

DECIPHERING DATA is a chapter about learning how to assess statistics, probability, and the validity of what other people tell us.

When we talk about deciphering data, we really mean how to interpret the world around us. Specifically, how can we interpret results, studies, charts, and conclusions that we are being told? If we see something in the newspaper, can we take it at face value or should we do our own digging and see what it actually means?

It's an important concept that is rarely covered because we rarely think it matters – we take others at face value even though they are subject to error and bias, just like any of us. This even includes scientists, reputable news outlets, and media sources. Often, they are even trying to push a narrative or achieve a goal with displaying data, so we can't always be so sure about our sources. There's no other way to explain the fact that two separate people can take one set of data and come up with two completely different conclusions.

People are typically trying to fit their agendas, it's important to understand the real story and to be able to poke holes in the data that you are presented.

In fact, people tend to be fooled by narratives that intuitively make sense to them in lieu of evidence (Bekker, 2013). This is human nature, but it is problematic for when you want to understand something without someone else's filter on it.

One of the easiest ways to do that is to take a look at some of the most common and widespread mistakes people tend to make with data and statistics, intentional or not. Hopefully after this chapter you'll develop a keener eye with which to pick apart what you're being presented, and ask the relevant questions that give you a clearer picture.

Correlation is Not Causation

Suppose that it's been found that ice cream sales happen to coincide with an increase of drownings at a local beach.

That's a mere correlation, or set of circumstances that happen to have occurred with the same increase or decrease. However, does a mere correlation mean that there was causation – that one of the factors caused the other? It might, but in no way can you say that it absolutely does.

Correlation is not causation. If I find that I am drinking three cups of coffee on days that I have a headache, that's a correlation that sounds like one element is causing the other.

And indeed, that's where most people falter, because there is absolutely no causation implied from the mere correlation. It's a mental leap that most of us will take because the premise and causation sound plausible enough to be true, and we don't look back once we decide it is indeed true.

Just because two things occur at the same time means absolutely nothing – it's as good as a coincidence without actual evidence to say otherwise. This is a prime way that innocent data can be presented to be twisted and misleading. Studies or presentations might seek to pair two things together and make them causal just because they happened to occur simultaneously or near each other. It means nothing unless you can prove with evidence that there is a predictable and reliable pattern, and you can reproduce the results consistently.

Confusing correlation for causation is also a sneakily lazy manner of dealing with data because it means you automatically eliminate any other possible explanation for the observed correlation. Just because both drowning and ice cream sales go up on the same day, is it wise to jump to that conclusion and rule out any other choices? There are literally an infinite amount of alternative conclusions, but you happen to settle on the one that is right in front of you. Sometimes this works, but most of the time it does not.

It might sound better if we drink three cups of coffee and get headaches each day it happens, but it's still a stab in the dark without testing it. That's the trap of confusing correlation with causation.

Correlation does not imply dependence, yet zero correlation does not imply independence.

The Gambler's Fallacy

The Gambler's Fallacy was actually covered earlier in the book as an obstacle to clear thought, but it might be even more relevant here.

As a reminder, the Gambler's Fallacy is essentially the feeling that there are predictable patterns in what are actually random and independent events.

For example, if you roll dice, you might feel that you should eventually roll a five because it's due time for it to happen. Never mind the fact that this is not statistically or probabilistically sound, you are attempting to create order in something which is impossible to have control over. They are completely independent events with no bearing on each other, and no pattern can be deduced as such. Even if you roll everything but a five a hundred times in a row, it doesn't make rolling a five any more likely the next time.

The Gambler's Fallacy is more so a fundamental misunderstanding of statistics and probability. And again, just like confusing correlation with causation, it's an incredibly easy trap to fall into because it just seems to *make sense*. But that's because we are thinking based on feelings and emotions, not based on the cold hard logic and facts.

This error of data interpretation occurs when we are too heavily influenced by past events, and we feel that they must influence future events. Even this is a statement that seems to be sound, but in the case of rolling the dice, the past event has no effect or influence on rolling the dice in the future. With independent and random events, there is no predictability to be found, and yet that's the reality of how the world works if we let go of the gut feeling we have about the Gambler's Fallacy.

This typically occurs to our detriment because we tend to use this type of thinking to predict that we are due for a positive outcome. Hence, the namesake of the gambler who is in trouble and yet keeps reaching for one last wager.

The solution to this error in data interpretation is to try to suss out whether you are concerned with random or truly connected events. If you are dealing with connected events, probability becomes involved. If you are dealing with independent events, you are depending on blind luck. Drawing cards from a deck is connected if you don't combine and shuffle the deck after, but it is decidedly random if you put the deck back the way it was before the first draw. It's a subtle distinction that we can miss quite easily.

Don't hunt for patterns where there are probably none, and if the probability doesn't clearly shift from event to event, you are probably depending on random luck. The Gambler's Fallacy has bankrupted many a person who felt that they were due a happy outcome, but they were just riding on luck.

Selection Bias

If I survey one hundred people on how much they like ice cream, are the hundred people truly random, or have I hand-picked them myself, or are they people I interviewed while standing in line at a popular ice cream store?

Selection bias is when the data you are presented is highly skewed and inaccurate because the data points involved aren't actually random. If you want to get an accurate read on how many people enjoy ice cream, you are introducing bias if you interview them in front of an ice cream parlor because it's the entire reason they were there.

It's not a random sampling of data, and thus the data is going to produce some very skewed and distorted results.

When you have such a bias inherent in a study, it means the results can't be generalized or transferred to any meaningful conclusion. You've just made it so that there's only one conclusion to be reached, and it's the one you were introducing. It's like using a word while trying to define it.

Usually, selection bias is done unconsciously so that we may receive the results we want, or we may avoid an outcome that makes us incorrect. If someone has invested a considerable amount of time into something, it's logical that they might hate that their time was wasted and manipulate the data to suit their needs.

However, I would like to think that most sources of selection bias are indeed unconscious, inadvertent, or merely oversight.

There are a few common ways that selection bias is introduced, skewing the results that you see. For example, someone might stop collecting data when the data indicates a conclusion they support. "I think we've got enough here, seems to be a fairly representative sample!"

They can also start to reject or include data for arbitrary reasons, unconsciously rationalizing a conclusion of their choice. "We better leave this one out, I just think it was a weird occurrence."

They might also discard and explain outliers to be unimportant and unrepresentative. "This person just didn't understand the question, obviously."

In fact, they might classify data points that go against their conclusion as outliers, and in doing so, eliminate up to 50% of the data. "All these people answered this way? No way. They just didn't get it. We've got to strike all of them."

For example, reviews of restaurants are highly skewed towards extremely good and extremely bad – neither of these are outliers, but selection bias could deem one side to be "unreasonable."

While you may not be present when someone justifies their selection bias, you would be smart to question people's methodologies and cast some healthy skepticism upon any biases they might be pursuing.

Margin of Error

What is a margin of error?

It's a term that is generally used whenever someone is describing the results of a survey or poll. For example, "These are what the polls predict, with a margin of error of plus or minus two percent."

That sounds nice, but what does it actually mean? Probably not what you think.

Let's take a polling situation for a local election of politicians. Pollsters would collect data from a small subset of voters in the city so they can try to project how the results will turn out. Obviously they can't poll that many people, so it's just a sample of the individuals that live there. And of course, this sample is bound to not match up with the actual results of the election simply because they can't ask everyone that lives there.

Margin of error is a term that measures the maximum amount by which the polls from the sample of individuals will differ from the election results involving the entire population. I won't go down the mathematical rabbit hole of discussing how to calculate a margin of error, because I'm not a mathematician and you probably don't care about it, you just want to understand how to interpret it.

Suppose you found that the 55% of the people sampled in a poll before the election said they would vote for candidate Bob.

If you are given a margin of error of two percent, you should feel quite confident the election overall will swing for candidate Bob, because at worst, 53% of the population at large will vote for him. Here, it doesn't matter because Bob has enough of the vote that the margin of error won't affect him. However, if only

50% of the people sampled in the poll indicated they would vote for Bob and the margin of error is still two percent, Bob will be sweating bullets until the results are announced.

Overall, the margin of error measures the accuracy of the sample population's opinions. It doesn't measure anything else.

Confusing Terms

Finally, I want to go over some confusing yet important terms when it comes to interpreting data. They are confusing because they typically have specialized meaning in the context of data and results.

Accuracy and Precision: In terms of deciphering and interpreting data, accuracy and precision are not synonyms. In fact, they mean something completely different in this context. Let's imagine that you are playing darts and there is a bulls-eye in the middle of your target.

Accuracy is how close to the bulls-eye your darts are, so it is an objective measure of performance.

Precision is how close your darts are to each other, so it is a measure of how consistent your performance is.

These terms are used interchangeably, but they are in fact not. You can have a result that is highly precise, yet entirely inaccurate, such as your darts hitting the same spot on the wall ten feet away from the dartboard.

Mean, Median, Mode: these numbers are all averages used to describe a set of numbers, and while some people use them interchangeably, they are incredibly different. They might occasionally converge and be the same, but that would be a result of pure coincidence. Make sure to specify which of these averages is being used so you can interpret data accurately.

The "mean" is the average that we are used to, where we add up all the numbers and divide by the number of numbers.

The median is the "middle" in a list of numbers – imagine you line up the numbers from smallest to greatest, and the median is the number that falls squarely in the middle.

The "mode" is the number that is the most frequently in the list.

Significance: In the realm of data, there are two types of significance: statistical significance and practical significance. Statistical significance is when the variables measured actually have some sort of causal relationship. Typically, a 5% chance of a causal relationship is notable enough to be deemed statistically significant, although it can depend on the context.

Practical significance essentially measures whether the results actually mean anything, and whether any actions can be taken to increase or decrease it. An outcome that is statistically significant may not be practically significant – it's actually quite common. If there is only a 5% relationship between two factors, it might not be worth your time to address. Always clarify which is being referred to, and always think to the next step of how you might act if something is practically significant. It asks what the implications and consequences are.

The final aspect of deciphering data and understanding what is really happening in front of you is dubbed the infinite monkeys theory, which is a take on probability. It states that if you could afford to wait until the end of time, a roomful of monkeys randomly tapping at typewriters would eventually completely reproduce a Shakespearian script.

This stands for the proposition that something, however likely, is technically possible. Don't be fooled and scared away if you're being told about the chances of something being a tiny probability. It might be possible, but what is the practical significance of concerning yourself with it? It would be like purchasing insurance for the highly unlikely event that a meteor smashes into the planet and decimates all of life.

There's simply nothing you should just accept at face value. You should always do your own homework.

11

Become an Idea Machine

PART OF BEING able to think effectively is being able to think your way out of problems with creative solutions that seem to appear out of nowhere.

However, underlying those solutions, and finding the right questions to ask to find those solutions, is simply the skill of having more and better ideas. Having more ideas and becoming an idea generating machine sounds something that seems so simple, but in reality, it's one of the hardest things in the world. It's doubly hard because we are never trained in such matters.

Here's a simple example: brainstorm five solutions to an improved version of an umbrella which doesn't break in the wind.

Got them? No?

Even though there is the old saying that ideas are a dime a dozen, ideas that *solve or address a particular problem* are far and few between. Ideas out of the blue addressed towards anything are easy, but useful ideas that can eventually be implemented are tough. This chapter covers a few effective idea generation tips, which you can also imagine as simply becoming better at brainstorming with yourself. As with creative thinking you'll find that the elements of what you need are often already inside of your mind, you just need the right question or approach to unlock them.

Quantity Over Quality

Sometimes, ideas just need to be blurted out. We can take it as a given that we have more genius inside us than we let out, but why do we keep it inside?

We often subconsciously filter most of what we say. It's usually because we are afraid of judgment, even when we are alone and no one can hear our thoughts. We stop ourselves prematurely by saying, "No, that's a stupid idea and it makes no sense." Even if it's true, it's the stupid ideas that make no sense that are like ladders to get to what you need. This is a point that may specifically rear its head in group brainstorming sessions, where one person is afraid to speak their mind and give voice to their ideas because they think it's inadequate, or that people will judge their idea for being useless. In the group setting, encourage safety and a lack of judgment, and accept everything without question or facial expression.

Brainstorming and idea generation is at its best when it is prolific, loud, unfiltered, and shameless. Shoot for quantity over quality, and blurt out the first things that pop into your head no matter what they are. They might not seem like steps forward, but they *help* you take steps forward toward the idea that will become your winner. Don't ruminate on the merits and negotiable aspects of an idea, just take every idea and keep moving.

Make it a game of how quickly you can get to a hundred ideas, and only then can you go back to edit and prune some of them. One hundred sounds like an impossible quantity, but the idea is for it to be so large that you start to think outside of the box and unconventionally just to fulfill the hundred. Often, the very best ideas come straight from the worst, and if you are trying to generate a hundred ideas, there will certainly be a few stinkers in there! You are wielding a shotgun here and just spraying and praying as widely as possible.

Which brings us to the next point.

Be Outlandish

Be outlandish, over the top, and increasingly crazy during your brainstorming phase. The reason this is so important is that you are stuck because you're thinking along conventional terms. You need to think differently, and intentionally embracing the outlandish and absurd will open you up to new possibilities and approaches.

When we approach a problem, we are usually solving for X. X is the problem we want to solve, and some combination of Y + Z is the solution. You probably aren't going to get far in generating ideas if you stick to the belief that the key is somewhere in Y or Z. You might want to experiment with A, B, or C, just to throw them in there and see what happens. It's a worthwhile way of thinking: introduce elements, think them through, and try to find exceptions, contradictions, or confirmatory evidence.

When you think outlandishly, it's the equivalent of working backwards. You pretend a theory works, and then you work backwards to see if it is proven wrong in any way.

Another benefit of thinking outlandishly is that you are intentionally reducing the logic and restrictions you have either put on yourself, or the situation has traditionally demanded. X = Y + Z occurred because you were following a set of rules and restrictions, but again, it's smart to momentarily act as if those restrictions don't exist so you can truly explore.

You'll read more about this approach later when we discuss exactly how Einstein stumbled upon the theory of general relativity he is so well known for. Just remember, each bad idea is a stepping stone to a good idea, and nothing is inherently without value.

Sprint

Sometimes, imposing a deadline or time limitation can be the best thing for your sense of ingenuity and creativity. The reason?

Something happens in our minds when we start approaching any kind of deadline. We start to embrace a certain kind of focus and alertness that is difficult to channel on command. For example, if you give yourself the task of coming up with as many ideas in ten minutes as possible, and then challenge yourself to keep beating your record in subsequent trials, the deadlines will be inherently motivating to you.

You'll lose all sense of a filter because you're competing against the clock and you aren't left to your own devices to be stuck in analysis paralysis. Just imagine how quickly you might answer questions and remove all filters if a gun was pointed at your head.

When you're in the heat of a tense moment like that, it's easy to blurt out what's on your mind because you want to act as quickly as possible. Your conscious filters are vetoed by your fear of the gun. Obviously, this is a different scale, but the feeling is similar. Staring down the face of a deadline can be very motivating and help you on your quest for quantity over quality.

The Snowball

The Snowball is named for what happens to a snowball when you roll it down a hill. It starts to accumulate more snow, and when it reaches the bottom of the hill, it is three times the size as when you started.

Imagine your initial snowball to be something you blurt out. As it rolls down the hill, keep adding to it in whatever way you can, such as asking what the implications are, how it will function, and what else will be involved. Add at least seven elements to that first idea. Then, you've reached your destination, take a step back and see what has been generated. Keep what seems to work and discard the rest, and do the same thing with the same idea again.

The Snowball works because you are lending focus to one idea at a time and fleshing it out further, no matter how zany or illogical it is. You are just devoting more attention to it, which makes you see it in a different way than from casually writing it on a piece of paper. It forces you to elaborate and add to something to make it plausibly workable.

If you are lucky enough to be with a group, or at least one other person, the Snowball works best because you can take turns adding to the same idea. When you alternate, you can both inject a fresh perspective, and what you will end up with afterwards is a collaborative Frankenstein monster of an idea – which is a good thing. You are shooting for depth versus breadth. Here, you are wielding a sniper rifle – going for depth and precision on a specific target.

Use the Alphabet

Here's where you are shooting for breadth. At the very least, you'll come up with twenty-six ideas when you use this method – one for each letter of the alphabet.

It's simple. For every letter, generate an idea related to your goal that starts with that letter. They don't have to be related or logical in any way, other than the fact that they have to start with a certain letter. If you can't make that work, start with having each letter in the first word of your idea or solution.

Psychological Distance

When we listen to our friends talk about their problems in their relationship or career, it all seems so simple, doesn't it? You know exactly what they want to do, even though they seem completely oblivious to it. It's not like you have phenomenal foresight or insight, you are just able to see what they don't see because they are too emotionally invested to think straight.

Indeed, when we rant and rave about our own problems to other people, we feel like there are no good solutions. Any direction we turn, there always seems to be additional considerations that muddy the waters. Every small detail and ramification is intensely magnified to us, so that even when our friends give us the best advice possible, we still shrug it off.

When we deal with our friends, we have psychological distance. We're not as involved, and we know it's not happening to us, so we can think clearly and come up with the right ideas. When we deal with ourselves, we have zero psychological distance. All of our ideas appear useless from that perspective because we're too emotionally involved.

Psychological distance is when you take subtle steps to make a question or problem seem farther away than usual, such as taking on someone else's perspective, or thinking of it as impossible, for the purpose of increasing the creativity and clarity you approach it with. Studies conducted at the Indiana University found that when you create psychological distance on something, it appears to be more abstract, while psychologically near things appear to be more concrete and personal.

A psychologically close representation of a book might be: blue, lightweight, smelling old, and on your bookshelf. However, a psychological distance representation of a book might be: knowledge, learning, helpful, useful, and educational.

Which of those descriptions of a book are more helpful for generating ideas and being creative? The abstraction that psychological distance creates makes it easier to connect unrelated ideas and create them out of thin air.

In recent studies also done at Indiana University, it was found that imagining something to be happening in Greece or California versus in Indiana produced very different answers as a result of psychological distance. In both cases, when the event was described to be occurring in farther locations, more ideas and problems were solved and generated. Because the problems were farther away and had no impact on their personal realities, they were easier to solve and think about.

In neither case did the geographic location matter to the idea or problem, but that slight change created a psychological distance to open up people's minds.

To generate more ideas, intentionally create psychological distance by thinking about the far future, far locations, and different realities and environments. Anything you are comfortable and familiar with, picture yourself in the opposite.

Sensory Deprivation

At special spas around the country, there are what are known as sensory deprivation tanks. What are in these tanks? Water and salt. And you won't even comprehend those when you're in there.

A sensory deprivation tank's purpose is to make it so that when you are inside, all five of your senses experience nothing. You receive zero stimulation. It is dark, you have earplugs, and you are floating in body-temperature water (the salt increases the water's density and makes your body buoyant) so even your sense of touch is nullified.

Sounds crazy, but sensory deprivation has been proven to result in extreme creativity. That's just what you might expect from something that has occasionally been known to cause hallucinations.

Why does sensory deprivation work? Essentially, when you are in a state of zero stimulation, your stress hormones decrease, and your pleasure hormones skyrocket. Then, your brain enters a state where it emits theta waves, a particular type of brain activity that is typically only engaged upon right before falling asleep and right after waking up. In other words, you're entering a kind of dream state where you are neither completely conscious nor unconscious.

Theta waves are theorized to contribute to our dreams, so they ostensibly provide vivid imagery and creative ideation. Sensory deprivation is a reliable way to enter this state of mind without continually napping and waking up. It's also been proven that when one part of the brain stops receiving input, other parts pick up the slack and contribute. This is where hallucinations enter the picture from a lack of sensory input from the eyes.

Sensory deprivation on a practical level will force your brain to wander because that's the only thing it can do.

You don't have to enter a fancy, expensive tank to achieve this goal. You can emulate this feeling at home with earplugs, blindfolds, isolation, and a temperature controlled room and environment. Try not to fall asleep and you will be pleasantly surprised with what you will be able to produce. It's the purest test of your creativity – to go one on one with your mind and see what you can squeeze out.

Steal

The final aspect of idea generation is to steal like a professional. There are in fact very few original ideas. Just take a second to search on Google how many food delivery companies there are in your state. Far too many.

Clearly, it's a good idea, and each food delivery company is doing something to differentiate itself and capture a different segment of the market. There might be a gourmet foods delivery company, an ice cream delivery company, an Asian delivery company, and so on.

The point is, even though these ideas are essentially the same, there are certain distinctions that make them stand on their own. They have taken one principle and adapted it to their industry or field.

Don't think of it as stealing. Think of it as borrowing and applying to your personal situation. Taking inspiration, even. It's the best form of flattery, after all. Plus, it's a skill in its own right to be able to see similarities and patterns between different scenarios, so you are cultivating multiple skills

An easy way to get started on stealing to generate ideas is to look at the problem you are trying to solve, and ask what perfect solution would solve it. Would it be the Amazon of your field, or the Apple of an adjacent field? Look at solutions and methods other people have used, and apply them for yourself. As I'm fond of saying, keep what works and discard what does not.

12

How to Develop Good Judgment

JUDGMENT IS the ability to come to a wise conclusion after having accurately weighed all of the factors involved.

Unsurprisingly, it's hard to come by. For many of us, it involves mental muscles we are not used to flexing. We want to go by our gut, hunch, or instinct. We rush decisions and don't look at all the factors. We assume we have complete information when it's nowhere close to that. We are influenced by our emotions, which can blind us from evidence staring us right in the face.

Yes, good judgment is difficult to attain. Another way to conceive of good judgment is that it is a combination of experience and knowledge – also difficult to attain, and necessarily involving large amounts of time.

Good judgment isn't necessarily genius thinking, but it's an imperative part of maximizing your life's enjoyment. This chapter contains a few of the keys to gaining better judgment and consistently making the right decisions for your life.

Balanced Viewing

Good judgment is a product of balanced viewing. That means that there is no fixation on the details, and there is no fixation on big ideas.

You need to be able to do both – multitask, so to speak. It is the description of the classic aphorisms, "He can't see the forest from the trees," and, "He can't see the trees from the forest." You can't be so focused on details that you lose sight of the overall goal.

This would be like devoting your time to picking out the wallpaper on a new house that is only half built. It's easy to get stuck on something small, trivial, or simple because it feels easy to do. It's actually a sense of procrastination most of the time.

Of course, you can't be so focused on the overall purpose that you glaze over details and consider them minor. This would be like being so pleased with the blueprint of the house you are going to build that you don't spend any time looking for a construction company and you choose the cheapest one available.

At either extreme, your judgment will be compromised because you don't have an accurate picture of what you are trying to accomplish. It's both. Sometimes, it is impossible to single-mindedly focus on one task at a time. Being able to do both will give you proper perspective and the ability to discern what actually matters, what needs work, and what can be skipped altogether.

Understand Deductive Reasoning

You are probably familiar with deductive reasoning because Sherlock Holmes, the famous detective, popularized it with the way he solved crimes. He could look at someone and immediately understand where they were and where they were going based on his observations. He put the pieces together into a narrative which was unfailingly correct, and the crime would be solved until the next installment.

More specifically, deductive reasoning is when you operate on hypotheses to make sense of data you find. For example, your hypothesis might be something like "the pool is wet," and "Mark was in the pool," which would lead you to deduce that Mark is wet. You take generalizations and turn them into specific observations.

Deductive reasoning basically allows you to skip the middle step of confirming that Mark is wet. You use the hypotheses, and if you take them to be true, it is likely that he was in the water.

We can break it down this way. A is true, and B is true. C is true when B is true. Therefore, C makes it likely that B is true.

People will typically use it to jump to incorrect conclusions, or conclusions that don't flow from the premises of A and B. For example, if "the pool is wet" and "Mark was in the pool", it lends itself to what would happen for one to cause the other. The real-world significance of understanding deductive reasoning is to be able to see when people are logically trying to put one over on you. It's easy to confuse the elements necessary for a real deductive conclusion.

Skepticism

Skepticism is the first step towards truth.

– Denis Diderot

Skepticism and doubt lead to study and investigation, and investigation is the beginning of wisdom.

– Clarence Darrow

What exactly is skepticism, and how does it help your judgment?

People with good judgment, by virtue of wanting to come to the best conclusion possible, never believe everything they hear. They are skeptical of what they come across – not because they rail against people's beliefs, but because they want to see evidence before endorsing or committing to the idea. They want to form their own opinions based on what they see, not just blindly follow others.

Your judgment will be vastly improved if you engage in healthy skepticism and hunt for knowledge on the path to your conclusion. It all comes down to this: what evidence is for or against a claim? Very little else matters; any way anyone else tries to dress up the evidence and facts is typically just a reflection of their bias or preference.

When you focus on the facts and evidence, you are able to make matters as black and white as possible and approach it like a scientist. Let's suppose my claim is that I was born on the planet Mars.

Has the claim been proven or verified in any other way? By anyone else? How convincingly, what was the margin of error, and what were the possible sources of error? There is no external, third-party proof or confirmation of my birth on Mars.

Has the claim been attacked by anyone, or is it merely being propped up by supporters? No one has gone out of their way to try to contradict my claim of being born on Mars. In fact, all sorts of Martian-supporting websites have rallied around me to show their support. This creates a strong confirmation bias that people are only seeing what they want to see – not a skeptical mindset, and not helpful for better judgment.

Does the claim have other possible explanations, or are they conveniently rationalized away? The alternate explanation is that I am either mentally disturbed or lying. Either are equally possible as the truth, but I usually dismiss people like that as liars. They have an agenda and they are out to get me!

Is the claim anything beyond anecdote? I started telling people about the origin of my birth when I was a kid, so it's really just from me. I have nothing to prove it, but there's nothing to prove it isn't true either. It's purely anecdotal, but just trust me.

Does the person making the claim have anything to gain from the claim? I do indeed come from a poor family and I have been thirsty for the spotlight of fame since I was a teenager. I have very much to gain because I could become rich and elevate my family's life to a life of luxury. My life would improve greatly if people believed I was born on Mars.

Those are the steps you can reliably follow to inject a bit of healthy skepticism into your life. It's a mindset that will lead you to ruffle feathers at times, but they likely aren't being ruffled because of you, it's because they know they are being exposed.

Recognize Your Own Bias

Though we are capable of acting rationally, it's certainly not our first instinct most of the time. Being aware of your own bias will increase your judgment because you will become more self-aware.

If you don't catch the biases, someone else will. When we talk about recognizing bias, we also mean growing our self-awareness. Self-awareness is the ability to what truly motivates your actions: the emotion and bias underneath.

The first step is to take stock and understand your life story. We all come from certain backgrounds and experiences related to that background. We are unique individuals, but still a byproduct of the environment we were raised in. It's our identity, whether we want to admit it or not – and our identity informs much of what we want in life and how we approach it.

A communist will approach a job differently than a capitalist, and a trust fund baby will think of vacations much differently than someone who was raised under the poverty line.

Who was your role model and how do you seek to emulate them to this very day? What formative experiences have informed how you perceive others, for better or worse? Have you had traumatic experiences and deaths in the family, or do you have a lesser concept of death and grieving? These all form our sources of bias. Our life stories make us unique, but also color our perception in a way that can be detrimental.

Second, try to see patterns in your life.

Patterns, in this context, are when you feel happy and when you feel sad. What puts you into those states? There's a good chance of uncovering your bias right there. If something has the power to launch you into strong emotions, it's going to affect how you view the world and the people that inhabit it.

Suppose you become enraged at the thought of people passing you in traffic. It means you probably have a sense of righteousness and justice that affects how you treat others. It's the seemingly small signs like this that belie our actions and motivations as a whole.

When we can recognize our bias, we inherently have better judgment because we can separate data into two categories: actual evidence, and everything else like bias, emotion, and narrative. It's not easy always to tell the categories apart. Good judgment is an amalgam of understanding what's in front of you and what to do next.

13

Solving for Relativity

HOW DID Einstein end up solving for the general theory of relativity, that which he is most famous and well-known for? It was a problem in physics that long-held theories dating back to Isaac Newton's time were beginning to fall apart with new discoveries that the turn of the twentieth century brought.

With these old models falling apart, it was imperative to find theories and models to integrate what we now knew about the universe, physics, and the inherent laws of nature.

Sometimes, geniuses really do think differently. Einstein in particular was known to think differently in one main way. He was never in the habit of writing down or verbalizing his thinking process, the major part of which was what he called *gedankenexperiments*, which is German for "thought experiment."

A thought experiment, in a more general context, is essentially playing out a "what if" scenario to its end. It's acting as if a theory or hypothesis was true, diving deep into the ramifications, and seeing what happens to your "what if" scenario under intense scrutiny. A thought experiment allows you to analyze interesting premises you could never do in reality, and make new leaps of logic and discovery because you can analyze premises that current knowledge doesn't yet reach.

For example, one of the most famous thought experiments is called *Schrödinger's Cat*, which was first proposed by physicist Erwin Schrödinger.

In his thought experiment, he sealed a cat inside a box along with two things: a radioactive element, and a vial of poison. There is a 50% chance that the radioactive element will decay over the hour, and if it does, then the poison will be released automatically to kill the cat. But in the 50% chance the radioactive element does not decay, the cat will remain alive. Because of the equal probabilities, it was argued that the cat was simultaneously alive and dead in the box. Without getting into the weeds too much, this is a clear paradox because it is impossible for something to be in two different states simultaneously, being dependent on a random molecular event that wasn't sure to occur.

In other words, the Schrödinger's cat thought experiment proved that there were constraints of current quantum physics theories, and certainly gaps in the knowledge of how they were to be applied. This never could have been something observable or testable, and a simple thought experiment was able to discover it.

Thought experiments were one of Einstein's superpowers. He could imagine a scenario, play it out mentally with shocking accuracy and detail, then extract the subtle conclusions that laid within. He almost certainly used a thought experiment to help piece together his understanding of special and general relativity. There were a few he used to make huge discoveries that contributed to his overall theories.

Riding a Beam of Light

In one of Einstein's most famous gedankenexperiments, it begins with the simple premise: what would happen if you chase and then eventually caught up and rode a beam of light through space? In theory, once you caught up to the beam of light, it would appear to be frozen next to you because you are moving at the same speed. Just like if you are walking at the same pace as a car driving next to you, there is no acceleration so the car would appear to be stuck to your side.

The only problem was that this was an impossible proposition at the turn of the century. If you catch up to the light and the light appears to be frozen right next to you, then it is inherently impossible to be light. It ceases to be light at that moment. This means one of the rules of physics were broken or disproved with this elementary thought.

Therefore, one of the assumptions that underlied physics at the time had to change, and Einstein realized that the assumption of time as a constant had to change. This directly laid the path for relativity. The closer you get to the speed the light, the more time becomes different for you – relative to your speed of travel.

A few elements were thought to be immutable and constant at that point in physics – time certainly was one of them.

This thought experiment allowed Einstein to challenge the convention and eventually challenge what was thought to be set-in-stone rules set forth by Isaac Newton's three laws of energy and matter. These were principles that were thought to be fact for two hundred years, and this thought experiment was instrumental in realizing that they may have been overbroad or subject to exceptions in extreme situations, such as traveling closer to the speed of light. People felt constrained trying to fit new information, data, and discoveries into old models, when they should have extended the old models and questioned them.

This thought experiment also allowed Einstein to fully explore an assumption and ignore what the models were telling him. All he wanted to do was solve the question of what the beam of light would look like, and the rest he worked out inside his head, independent of the accepted models of physics. He wasn't searching to confirm or contradict anything, he just wanted to answer his own questions, and as a result, played a "what if" game that broke some very fundamental rules. The evidence dictated his answers, not adhering to theories or models.

Einstein had a plethora of famous thought experiments, but he used another to prove his major points about the theory of relativity.

Standing on a Train

This gedankenexperiment was instrumental in demonstrating that someone in motion literally has a different reality than someone standing still.

Imagine you are standing on a train, while a colleague is standing at a stationary point nearby watching the train pass them by. Now suppose that lightning strikes both the front and the back of the train simultaneously. Your colleague would see the lightning strike at the same time from their stationary point.

However, that is not true if you are standing on the train. You will see the lightning bolt the train is traveling toward first because it has a shorter distance to travel – the lightning bolt at the front of the train.

This was another piece of the puzzle that space and time function relatively, and there is no true objective measure.

There were obviously many other parts that went into Einstein solving for relativity, including a rivalry with the top mathematician at the time, and also the convergence of new data and discoveries when Einstein was coming of age.

However, the gedankenexperiment is an important concept to become familiar with. It can lead you to a discussion and discovery about something that seems like a quantum leap of progress because it's something you couldn't necessarily make a connection to from current science.

You can be stuck at point A, but investigate what you might think about point Z, and in doing so, work out what parts of what happens in-between.

If you want to test a theory, a thorough thought experiment will show you what may actually happen, and then you can make your theories from that, instead of the other way around. Many people have the tendency to want to make reality conform to their theories, but the thought experiment does the opposite – theory from observation and testing reality. To some, that might be more logical.

Conclusion

BY THE WAY, to finish the riddle from the introduction of this book, Janet and Daniel weren't human. They were fish, so the water and glass was from a broken aquarium. Somehow, the aquarium was broken, and the fish died as they ran out of oxygen.

Didn't expect to change that parameter, did you?

Cultivating critical thought is always the toughest thing to do because you are fighting years of instinct and evolution that have told you to rely on your gut emotion. We're also lazy by default, so for people like me, critical thinking is always a struggle.

I sometimes think back to that day of agony, pre-internet, where I couldn't look up the answer. It was just my mind versus the riddle and the riddle was getting the best of me. It was such a frustrating feeling, especially when I discovered that the answer was literally right in front of me.

You've read just the kind of difference training your brain can make in the kind of results you have, and ways you can avoid deception whether intentional or not. Sharpening your insight isn't just about being more observant or solving logic riddles. That might be where it starts, but it can have a very real positive effect on your life.

And you don't have to be a mathematician to reap the rewards.

Best of luck,

Peter Hollins

Summary

Chapter 1. Obstacles to Clarity of Thought

Though there are many obstacles to thinking clearly and effectively, there are four main ones covered in this chapter. Inertia and sloth, incorrect logic (1 + 1 = 3 on accident), incorrect perception (1 + 1 = 3 on purpose), and rigid thinking.

Chapter 2. Three Frameworks of Thinking

There are three primary frameworks covered in this chapter, the Facione Model, the RED Model, and the Paul-Elder Model of critical thinking. There are many commonalities when you compare these frameworks to the classic scientific method.

Chapter 3. Creative Problem Solving

A few ways of creative problem solving include finding the problem's essence, committing and producing, combining different concepts, making outlandish assumptions, and role playing to think in different ways.

Chapter 4. The Socratic Method

The Socratic Method is the art of asking important questions to highlight a lack of understanding. There are six different types of questions, each with a different shortcoming to highlight.

Chapter 5. Making Smarter Decisions

There is no perfect choice – there is usually only a choice that will be most of what you want, and the rest will be diminishing returns. You can apply predetermined filters, and also have a default while you are wallowing in analysis paralysis.

Chapter 6. Find Your Intelligence Type

There are eight intelligence types: linguistic, logical, visual, kinesthetic, musical, interpersonal, intrapersonal, and naturalist.

Chapter 7. Priming the Engine

The engine of your brain should be taken care of as if you were an athlete getting ready to compete. Relaxing and doing nothing, eliminating stress can be surprising sources of inspiration, while sleeping right, eating right, and following your particular circadian rhythm help your overall brain health.

Chapter 8. Memorize More

Your memory has a specific structure, and methods such as spaced repetition, mnemonics, flashcards, metaphors, and stories can help memories take the leap from working memory into long-term memory.

Chapter 9. The Mozart Effect, Chess, and Brain Training

Three myths surrounding increasing the brain's performance. Are they true? No. The Mozart Effect has never been reproduced, training yourself in chess increases individual skills but not overall brain capacity, and brain training companies have been sued as fraudulent.

Chapter 10. Deciphering Data

The data, statistics, and probabilities we are presented with on a daily basis are typically misleading or incorrect. You can learn to make your own decisions by understanding correlation/causation, the Gambler's Fallacy, selection bias, and margins of error.

Chapter 11. Become an Idea Machine

To generate more ideas, you can use the alphabet, create psychological distance, use sensory deprivation, and steal ideas from other domains.

Chapter 12. How to Develop Good Judgment

Keys to better judgment are understanding impact versus detail, seeing deductions, embracing skepticism, and discovering your own biases.

Chapter 13. Solving for Relativity

Einstein solved for relativity on the basis of his famous thought experiments, *gedankenexperiments* in German. The two most famous though experiments were "riding a beam of light, and "standing on a train."

Learn Like Einstein

2
BOOKS
IN 1

Learn Like Einstein

2 BOOKS IN 1

Peter Hollins

JAICO PUBLISHING HOUSE

Ahmedabad Bangalore Chennai
Delhi Hyderabad Kolkata Mumbai

Published by Jaico Publishing House
A-2 Jash Chambers, 7-A Sir Phirozshah Mehta Road
Fort, Mumbai - 400 001
jaicopub@jaicobooks.com
www.jaicobooks.com

Published in arrangement with
Peter Hollins
1112 Eddy Street Unit C
San Francisco, California 94109, USA

To be sold only in India, Bangladesh, Bhutan,
Pakistan, Nepal, Sri Lanka and the Maldives.

LEARN LIKE EINSTEIN
ISBN 978-93-86867-76-6

First Jaico Impression: 2018
Fifth Jaico Impression: 2025

Page design and layout: R. Ajith Kumar, Delhi

Printed by
Trinity Academy For Corporate Training Limited, Mumbai

Contents

Introduction

When I was younger, I was never at the top of my class.

I didn't know how to study or learn. I would rush at the last minute to cram and pull all-nighters on projects that I had months for. I would take terrible notes and rely on my friends to help me out. I even skipped class somewhat frequently.

Okay, I was a downright bad student. I just didn't care, and would rather have spent time riding my bike.

However, something happened in eighth grade that would change my world forever.

I wanted to impress *Jessica from Spanish class*. It's a noble and mighty motivation that has been the impetus for many changes in the life of a young (and old) male. We were in the same Spanish class and I had the good fortune of sitting directly behind her. It turns out she wasn't too interested in Spanish either, so she would constantly turn around and ask me for help.

I would first get caught in her eyes, but then my spirits would fall because I realized I had no idea how to answer her questions. What if she started asking the other guys in the class? I didn't want that!

With that in mind, I began to study and learn Spanish so she would have all the more reason to continue turning around and talking to me. It's amazing what you can do when you have the proper motivation for it, and I probably became fluent more quickly than anyone in the class that year. What's more, I would look up obscure or complex phrases and words to impress her, just in case I had the opportunity.

I mainly used a massive set of flashcards. They started with one word on the back of each card, but by the end of the school year, they had three to four sentences on back of each, all in Spanish. I got an A+ in the class, one of my few in my academic career, but I never did get anywhere with Jessica.

Still, I had discovered that when you have an overarching goal or purpose in mind, you can accomplish far more than you would expect. It worked for me.

Most of the time in life, we don't have this type of motivation that drives us to achievement. Most of the things we learn or study for, we drag our feet towards. It's not a pleasure, and it's more of a chore. Studying and learning isn't typically fun.

What do we do then? What do we do when it feels like a struggle to crack open that book or listen to that lecture?

Learn Like Einstein is designed just for you. This book is a collection of learning techniques that are guaranteed to make you retain more and learn faster, even if you hate what you're looking at. You still may not be happy that you're learning or studying at all, but at least you'll accomplish more in less time, and be able to move on to other activities sooner rather than later.

Learning to learn is one of the most valuable skills you can equip yourself with, because anything worthwhile in life is a result of effective and efficient learning techniques.

1

Shattering Myths

WELCOME TO *Learn Like Einstein*, where the good become great, the great become legendary, and the mediocre become less mediocre!

That may have sounded like hyperbole, but I assure you it's not. Learning how to learn is one of the biggest superpowers anyone can have under their belt. You might not realize it, but learning to learn will unlock just about everything you do in life.

Why? The simple reason that we aren't born as experts – in anything!

When you entered the world as a baby, you didn't know anything on your own, so you first depended on social learning to pick up how to eat, drink, walk, and talk. Everything that we take for granted is something that we learned from others.

The first five years of life are a wash because everyone learns out of necessity. Everyone learns to walk, talk, swallow, and tie their shoelaces. But what about after? You start to see people separate themselves from the pack. Josh can do the multiplication and division tables faster than his teacher, so he gets to skip a grade. Josiah, however, is still having trouble with subtraction so he is held back a grade.

Is it because Josh is inherently smarter? Not necessarily. In fact, that's something we'll address in this chapter and throughout the book.

It's all due to learning, and how each child learns to learn. Then, as we grow older, we start to see people become outliers and separate themselves even more as a result of their talent in learning, not necessarily talent in the underlying subject.

Being that this chapter is about learning myths, that's a good place to start.

Myth #1: Innate intelligence matters in learning.

This took some careful phrasing, because there are indeed some outlier geniuses such as Einstein and Newton that simply think on a different level. However, they are so rare that if you took a minute, you probably wouldn't be able to come up with more than a handful of famous "geniuses." What about the rest of us?

Intelligence is a very, very hazy term. For example, IQ tests claim to measure intelligence (it's right in the name, after all), but they only measure a small set of very specific metrics that they think translates into intelligence. Classic IQ tests measure things like ingenuity, thinking outside the box, seeing patterns, and making connections.

These are good qualities, but as you can see, not quite what would qualify someone to be categorized as intelligent. They don't take into consideration a whole world of factors.

For the purposes of learning, no one is more intelligent or better than anyone else. Learning is something we've all done since we were children, and it's really a matter of work, attention, and some of the principles in this book that take your learning ability to the next level, not your innate talent or intelligence.

Your overall intelligence and learning ability is truly measured by far more factors that can ever be seen in any test results. You can learn just as well as anyone else, and if someone else appears to understand something more quickly, they are simply seeing it through a different perspective, not dissecting it like a genius.

If you don't believe that you are can do something as well as someone else, then why try at all? It's actually a very dangerous assumption that others are simply

innately better at something, because it will cause a very real sense of discouragement and pointlessness.

Myth #2: Failure is bad.

Actually, studies have proven that failure is one of the best things that can happen during the learning period.

Allowing someone to fail, even when you can easily help them, is great for learning as well. This concept is called "Productive Failure" that a researcher from the University of Singapore coined. There were two groups of students, and teachers helped the first group find answers to their set of problems. Meanwhile, the second group was given no help, but was instructed to collaborate and work with each other.

The second group didn't actually answer any of the problems correctly, but as a result of working together to come up with different approaches, they had a far greater understanding of what solutions could and should look like, and what was involved in generating it. When the groups were compared in terms of what they had learned, the second group "significantly outperformed" the first.

What does this tell us about learning?

Simply giving someone the answer and making sure they never fail is massively detrimental to their learning. It robs us of the critical thinking and analysis

that we need to learn better. The struggle for answers is what truly aids our sense of learning.

The Singaporean study also identified three specific conditions that promoted productive failure. First, failure is best when it promotes a sense of challenge and engagement versus frustration. Frustration, of course, is the feeling that you are going nowhere at top speed, so there has to be a sense of progress and achievement. You can't just hand a child a calculus equation and expect productive failure. It has to be within their capabilities and they have to be able to see improvement.

Second, failure is best when learners have the opportunity to elaborate on what they are doing and thinking, as was done in a group setting during the study. When you can narrate what you're doing, instead of toiling away in silence, it can help shed light on your efforts because you're actively thinking about what you're doing and analyzing it. Often, thinking out loud leads to solutions that wouldn't have appeared otherwise.

Third, failure is best when learners have the chance to compare solutions that work, and solutions that don't. This is what happens when you aren't shown the exact path every single time. You recognize the red flags of failure and gain intuition when something seems right or wrong.

You could call this a "tough love" approach to learning. Give a man a fish, feed him for a day, but teach a man to fish (while letting him struggle with it himself for a bit), feed him for a lifetime. Allowing failure is when you teach the skill of problem solving, which is another way to define learning at large.

Myth #3: If you forget, you lose.

We have a conception of memory and learning that if we forget something, even momentarily, it's a sign that we didn't do a good job learning it in the first place.

That's not true. In fact, forgetting is an essential part of the process of creating new memories. It's a filter for unimportant information: we forget what we don't use or need. Everything we hear or see is headed towards the road of forgetting until we realize that we need or want the information – then we access it from our memory banks.

What makes us realize that we want or need the information? We rehearse or access it repeatedly. It's this accessing, sometimes called active learning, that actually cements the information into our memory. When the brain has to work hard to retrieve something that may be half-forgotten already, the strength of that memory is correspondingly increased.

Myth #4: More is better.

You've no doubt seen this in action with people who study all day and night, and cram the night before the exam as well. Is the greater amount of hours spent studying a better method of retaining information? Not always.

It's just too much, and while it may not necessarily be detrimental to your learning and memory, it sure isn't helping. Studies have shown that a concept known as spaced repetition is far more effective for learning and memory than daily rote memorization.

This means the brain is like a muscle, and it simply needs time to recover and make neural connections for the information that you've consumed. It also means that if you overdo it and burn out, you are wasting time by attempting to learn more than your brain can handle at the time. Then, you encounter the phenomenon where you are reading the same paragraph over and over and don't comprehend it.

Finally, it places an emphasis on memorization versus understanding and analysis, the latter of which is what will help information stick in your brain the best. More isn't better; smarter is better.

Myth #5: "I'm just a left-brain person!"

There is a myth that since the brain hemispheres do have certain proclivities towards creativity versus logic,

that people should target their learning to cater to these differences.

For example, right-brain people are supposed to be more creative, free-flowing, and carefree, while left-brain people are supposed to be more logical, analytical, and deliberate. It can certainly be a romantic myth to buy into, but it doesn't mean you learn with just one side and that side should be appealed to exclusively.

Both brain hemispheres are involved in almost every single mental process, and studies have demonstrated that people do not have dominant hemispheres whatsoever. What does this mean for you? Just because you're more artistic or more analytical doesn't mean that you should ignore the other parts of life! You can be equally as good at those parts, if not better, so don't let the myth of the dominant hemisphere prevent you from exploring other areas.

Imagine the problems that occur when you focus too deeply on one hemisphere's proclivities: you may be cutting yourself severely short, and you may not diagnose yourself correctly.

Now that we've gotten a few myths out of the way and hopefully feel a bit more empowered and encouraged as to our learning abilities, it's time to dive in and learn the foundations of learning better.

2

Foundations for Better Learning

THE FOUNDATIONS for better learning are what put your mindset into a space where you are ready to receive and process as much information as possible.

The important word here is "mindset", as it starts with a concept called "growth mindset". Researcher Carol Dweck has done multitudes of research on the topic, and she found that most people have either a *growth* or *fixed* mindset.

People with fixed mindsets believe that intelligence and learning ability is innate and determined by genetics. People with growth mindsets believe that intelligence and learning ability is a result of effort and hard work, despite genetic fate. This is an extension of the myth we discussed in the first chapter, the notion that you have a genetic cap to your abilities.

In subsequent studies, Dweck found that people with fixed mindsets tended to learn far worse, because they believed that if they weren't instantly proficient at something, they were genetically destined to be bad at it. Success was a sign of where they should focus their efforts, and failure was a sign of something to be avoided, as they didn't feel that they could improve at it. People with growth mindsets, on the other hand, approached new topics with an expectation of struggle and challenge, and knew from their past experiences that hard work could help them overcome what appeared to be impossible at first.

When you believe that you will face struggle and require work to reach a level of proficiency in anything, you can imagine how this affects the way you learn and grow comfortable outside of your comfort zone. A growth mindset creates the optimistic belief that you can achieve just about anything with hard work and time.

One of the foundations to better learning is the belief that you *can* learn better.

The next foundation is to understand the pyramid of learning, which you'll see traces of throughout this book. Many people have questioned the accuracy of the pyramid, but I would argue that it's not meant to be taken as an exact number, rather a useful guideline that demonstrates that really matters in retaining knowledge.

The pyramid is as follows:

- You retain 5% when you hear a lecture
- 10% when you read
- 20% from audio visual processing
- 30% from demonstrating [this and up are demonstration methods]
- 50% from group discussion [this and below are participatory methods]
- 75% from practice by doing
- 90% from teaching others

As you can see, the exact numbers may not be that important, but the differences in style are telling. The middle few might differ for many people, but the ends of the spectrum are absolutely true. The more you proactively process and participate in the analysis of information, the better you will retain and learn it. The more passively you intake information without a second thought, the less you will retain and learn. Would you learn more from surfing for two hours, or watching a movie about surfing?

Let's take two examples: one physical and one mental, to see how this works in real life.

If you want to learn how to ski, you aren't going to learn much from a lecture or reading. You might learn

about the mechanics and why certain actions matter, but you won't actually be able to ski unless you do it. You demonstrate it for others, then receive immediately feedback, and you practice by doing so you can apply what you've learned. Obviously, for a physical act, we can see that learning is almost non-existent without moving down the spectrum toward active participation and analysis.

And now for the mental example.

If you want to learn more about the history of Spain, you might learn a good deal just from passively processing the information. You could take notes, re-read your notes, watch a documentary on Spanish conquistadors and Christopher Columbus, and easily be considered well-read on the topic.

However, imagine how much more you would gain if you were to dissect with others the motivations of the Spanish Inquisition, or create a video to demonstrate just how Columbus sailed across the Atlantic Ocean. Further, imagine if you practiced rehearsing a speech about Spanish history that was meant to teach your co-workers. Finally, imagine that your co-workers were all Spanish, so they were going to pepper you with questions that you had to prepare for.

It's a different level of learning that occurs when you roll up your sleeves and really analyze a topic versus simply reading it. Remember, while the pyramid of

learning isn't 100% accurate, it's accurate at the top and bottom levels, which create important distinctions in learning technique.

The next foundation to better learning is to understand focus. The attention and energy we can put toward learning is our most valuable resource because it's the most limited. We might have all weekend, but we might run out of attention span or energy to learn by Saturday afternoon. Therefore, we have to learn to extend our attention span and focus a bit better for better learning.

The first step in better focus is to give up your attempts at multi-tasking.

This could easily have been covered in the first chapter about myths, but I felt it fit better when talking about the quest for focus. When you attempt to multi-task, your focus, attention, and energy is spent switching between your tasks and re-orienting yourself to exactly where you were before you switched. It's like swimming against the current. Every time you take a stroke, you might only get one quarter of a stroke forward because of the current, and sometimes you might even go backwards despite your best efforts.

It's an inefficient use of your time that ends up in your becoming well-versed in the beginning stages of many tasks, but never quite seeing them to completion.

The better approach is to be willfully ignorant

of everything else you need to do, while giving full attention to one task at a time. In a sense, a lumberjack can only chop the tree in front of him or her, and can't do anything with a bunch of half-chopped trees. Chopping the tree in front of you will allow you to make better progress on everything more than actively working on it while multi-tasking. It's counterintuitive yet true.

The next step is to proactively prevent procrastination, and you can do this in a few ways. You can visually clear your workspace so nothing catches your attention and distracts you. You can impose a "one-touch" rule, which means the first time you see or touch a task is the moment you take care of it to completion. This is easier said than done. Finally, you must beware of what I like to call the trap of productive procrastination.

It's when we suddenly feel the need to vacuum our carpets or clean our bathrooms right when we have real work to do. It doesn't feel like a waste of time because in theory you are doing something positive and productive. However, it doesn't help your overall goal, and only assists you in avoiding something else. It may not be the worst habit, but it's something we don't realize we're doing to simply avoid more urgent or difficult work.

The final step to better focus is to pay attention to your attention. What do I mean by this?

Think of your attention like a muscle. You can't overwork it, and there is a limit as to what you can do with it on a daily basis. You can also train it to be bigger and better, and there are certain things that improve and discourage it. You can give it breaks and you can also recharge it.

The biggest takeaway should be that your attention is a limited quantity. You have to preserve it for the tasks that you need to get done. Whether this means saving it by avoiding other tasks, or preemptively removing temptation for your attention (such as television or objects to fiddle with) from your surroundings, you need to treat it like a battery that runs down throughout the day.

You can't learn well when your attention levels are shot, so take care to pay attention to your attention before you start, and during your learning. Sometimes you can't force yourself to push through, and that's okay.

The end goal of all of these foundations is to set ourselves up for success, and success has been conveniently defined for these purposes by Noel Burch in the four levels of competency.

The four levels of competency are:

- Unconscious competence – We have incorrect intuition about what we're learning because we don't understand it at all.

- Conscious incompetence – We have incorrect analysis about what we're learning, because we only know some of the ground rules.
- Conscious competence – We have correct analysis but not habits or intuition yet, as we're only getting started with successful application of the ground rules.
- Unconscious competence – We have correct intuition about the future because we have seen and analyzed the application of the ground rules enough that we can understand what will happen before it happens.

The same examples from before clearly illustrate these levels of competency. You can only learn to ski when you understand the ground rules and develop habits to apply them, which gives you instinctual habits when you're skiing down a slope that is new to you. Likewise, you might understand Spanish history, but if you take the trends and analyze them, you can explain why certain events occurred and justify the current Spanish position in Europe.

Be aware that unconscious competence is where some people start from, and it's dangerous because they typically make terrible teachers because of their inability to explain their reasoning not based on a gut feeling.

The levels of competency and creating intuition mirror the true learning process in a nutshell:

1. Try

2. Achieve or fail

3. If you fail, analyze failure

4. Go to step one.

Where this process can go wrong is the following:

1. Try

2. Achieve or fail

3. If you fail, ***analyze failure incorrectly or fail to correct actions.***

4. Go to step one.

The pyramid of learning, four levels of competency, and better focus all contribute to ensuring that you don't fall into the trap of the second, failing process.

3

Know and Understand Thyself

THE FIRST and foremost step to being better at learning is to know thyself. What that means is to know and understand exactly how you learn and process information the best.

This may come as a surprise to some that people have very different preferences of how they learn. There are studies that show greater increased efficacy when exposed to a style or preference that best suits them.

You don't need to take these guidelines as hard evidence, but the simple realization that you can engage information in different ways should greatly influence the way you learn. You might feel stuck in one way, only to shift to another medium and discover that it works much better for you. You might feel great in one

method, shift to another and find that it takes you to the next level.

The point is to have more ammunition in your learning arsenal. If you were in a learning competition with someone else, and they could unleash all their learning potential, because they understood the three best types of information they responded to or knew how to engage themselves in three different ways, you will lose hands down if you have only stuck to one your entire life, even if you're great at it and have it down to a science.

Think of it as if you only spoke French, yet you were forced to read all your news and watch television in Russian. After a few years you might be pretty good at it, and you might even be have methods that work for you, but you'll never be as proficient or efficient than if you could read and watch in French.

That's what not understanding your best learning styles and preferences is like, and that's the risk you run.

Let's get down to it. In this chapter, I only describe two of the main models of learning.

There are many more, but these are among the most widespread and prevalent. They further demonstrate that learning and expertise is not a one size fits all approach, and really, it can't be unless you are simply shooting for minimum competency. Remember,

while we go through everything presented, try to ask yourself if it sounds like something you might enjoy or something you might hate. Both distinctions are important to make.

The VARK Model of Learning

VARK is an acronym that stands for the four types of learning it splits people into. It was developed by Neil Fleming. The four types of learning are:

- Visual
- Auditory
- Reading/Writing
- Kinesthetic

If you have a visual style of learning, it means you prefer to see information so you can actually visualize concepts and how they may or may not connect with others. Try to summarize information in charts, graphs, or even pictures that get the point across in little to no time. At the very least, you can organize notes and information in a way that is visually organized for better absorption. Information that is merely heard or read just doesn't make the same impact, and tends to go in one ear and out the other.

If you have an auditory style of learning, it means you like to hear information rather than see or read it.

Hearing is the best way for you to process information because it allows you to process that information simultaneously with your own internal train of thought. Reciting information out loud is also helpful because it's an active and conscious act, not like when others do it. It allows you to think out loud and come to conclusions and connections yourself, where you wouldn't be able to through reading or writing. To work best, record people as much as possible, including yourself, and think out loud to find your conclusions.

If you have a reading and writing style of learning, you prefer to interact with text and manipulate it. It allows you to process information thoroughly and at your own pace.

Reading over notes and making summaries of those notes will work best for you, and tactics such as mindmaps also help, because they clearly allow you to make connections between concepts. To work best, you should always ask for a written copy, then annotate it yourself with your own notes and thoughts. That way, you can draw your own conclusions and see the evidence right before you.

If you have a kinesthetic learning style, you can't sit still for a lecture or lesson, and you want to experience the topic at hand. You need to try, poke around, and discover for yourself the inner workings of something because simply being told doesn't make much of an impression. You need exercises and problems to solve,

trivia to name, and worksheets to fill in. This is the epitome of proactive learning, and it's no surprise that the kinesthetic learning style is effective for many people whether they realize it or not. It forces participation and active analysis, which is best for memory creation and retention. You work best through seeing demonstrations, then doing them for yourself to pick up anything you might have missed otherwise.

The Seven Learning Styles

The Seven Styles bear quite a few similarities to the VARK model of learning. There is actually overlap in the types of mediums that are mentioned, and for good reason: there are five senses and you can only appeal to them in so many ways. However, where the VARK model seems more conventional and concrete, the seven styles is more geared towards people's innate preferences and talents.

Without further ado, below are the seven styles of learning:

- Visual/Spatial
- Aural
- Verbal
- Solitary
- Social

- Logical
- Physical

Visual learning styles prefer to see pictures, images, movies, and are generally be able to visualize whatever they are learning directly. You will see through descriptions of the other learning styles that visual learners process information better with their eyes. Seeing something with your eyes is what cements it in your brain. Even if you are reduced to reading or listening, you can replace the words with pictures, use bold colors to highlight areas of importance, and make your notes and outlines easy to visually comprehend. Suppose that you still want to learn the history of Spain. You'd be best suited to studying nautical maps, graphics, charts, seeing movies, and any other visual media that keeps you from having to solely read or listen. Turn your lecture notes into diagrams that hold a lot of information, and make it so you can digest information from a single glance at your page.

Aural learners are also known as musical learners. This is important to distinguish, because the VARK method tends to lump them in together with auditory learners. Aural learners don't necessarily prefer listening for better learning, they prefer everything that underlies the appeal of their favorite music. Rhythm, patterns, rhyme, and melody. These are the people that will hum incessantly and make songs for themselves to memorize

facts and dates. You might imagine this to be a small minority of learners, but in reality, this exists in all of us. It's why we sometimes can't get commercial jingles out of our heads. To better learn Spanish history, you would do your best to work information into existing or new songs and melodies, because they come to you easily and the information will be secondary to the music – which is a good thing.

Verbal learners are also known to be linguistic learners, which means they not only prefer words spoken out loud, they prefer to read as well. This type of learner has it easy at first glance because most of the information that is readily available is in book or lecture form. To learn better, you take what you've heard or read and write it out yourself to strengthen the connections within. To learn Spanish history more effectively, you would take a series of sample test questions and write the answers out and let the insight flow from your pen. If you prefer to use words, you should stick to words and boil any diagrams, graphics, or pictures down to simple descriptions that you can dive into with more detail later. Copious, organized notes that are scribbled over again and again would be normal for this type of learner. You should do your thinking out loud in written form and write questions for yourself to answer later.

Solitary learners represent a point of significant departure from the VARK model, which focused on

the types of input that you could receive. The seven learning styles are more holistic definitions that focus on how you best process information. Solitary learners prefer to work alone and process their thoughts by themselves. Everything happens in their own head, and they create their own materials and methods for self-study. They may interact with others, but when it gets down to the wire, they withdraw into a cave with themselves to make connections for themselves. They know what questions to ask themselves and where their knowledge gaps lie. When others explain concepts, it just doesn't have the same impact – they need to think through it step by step for themselves. To learn Spanish history better, the solitary learner would hunker down in a bunker, alone for days with a few textbooks and lectures.

The social learner is predictably the opposite of the solitary learner. They prefer to learn in groups, or with other people, so they can bounce ideas and concepts off them. They want to seek as wide a set of perspectives as possible because that will increase their overall understanding. They prefer to see variety, breadth, and diversity of opinion because that will leave no stone unturned. After confirming their questions or beliefs, they can then be confident in what they've learned. To learn Spanish history better, the social learner would engage in a series of role play or Q&A group study sessions where the information comes out in answers and not through strict reading.

The logical learner prefers to learn through making logical connections and seeing the underlying systems and reasoning. This is the type of person that likes math because there is a single correct method that, if followed, will yield a single correct answer. There is no uncertainty and almost everything can be explained in some logical manner. You would search for the motivations that create action, because understanding the entire context will help with learning the logic. To learn Spanish history better, the logical learner looks at the big picture context of why certain events occurred and the series of events that took place afterward as a consequence. You want to make sense of the world by being able to say, "Oh, that's why that happened. That's the rule," even though it's not always possible.

The physical learner prefers actual, physical stimulation for learning. To touch is to experience, and to experience is to know. Using their kinesthetic sense cements information because they are tied to strong feelings and emotions. Sitting stationary in a chair is the worst scenario for this type of learner. They'd much rather get up and interact with others, create materials, interact with demonstrations, role-play, and use their five senses as much as possible. They want to feel, which transmits stronger memories to them. To learn Spanish history better, the physical learner would prefer to explore with their hands as much as possible in museums, folk dance demonstrations, creating

models or charts about Spanish history, and have group performances in front of an audience.

This chapter presented two models of learning, with eleven separate ways of processing information. Which ones resonated with you, and which felt like ones you'd ignore as much as possible? Most people are a mixture of multiple methods, so you may take elements from a few of the eleven methods presented. What's important is to know yourself and construct a method of learning that best suits your preferences and needs. Only then can you begin to learn like Einstein.

As a final point, there has been increasing scrutiny and criticism about the validity of learning styles. Namely, that despite what people deem their styles or preferences to be, it makes no difference as to the overall retention of information.

Is this true? It may very well be. However, learning will always involve sitting still for extended periods of time, something people can withstand for only varying degrees. Therefore, it might be more helpful and empowering to view each learning style or preference as a tool or trick to make learning more captivating, relatable, or motivating than sitting quietly at a desk by themselves.

4

Faster and More Efficient Reading

WITHOUT A doubt, becoming a better reader is tantamount to becoming better at learning.

You might hate reading, or it might be the opposite of your learning style and preferences, but you're not going to be able to avoid it. Most of your initial consumption of information is going to come through the written word, especially if you are taking your learning into your own hands. What you do with the information after you've consumed it is up to you, but you're still going to start any new learning venture by reading voraciously and consuming as much as possible.

It's the initial gatekeeper that prevents most people from getting into their learning groove. They'll look at

a new book or even series of articles and determine it would take them too long to finish, so what's the point? The sense of instant gratification is destroyed when you read slowly or ineffectively. Learning about something new will appear to be a boulder of a task.

That's why becoming a better reader is so important. It's the first step that you'll have to take whenever you want to learn something new.

Being better at reading generally has three parts that I'll cover in more detail: speed, efficiency, and how much is retained.

Reading Faster

For most people that haven't studied speed reading on an individual level, attempting to read too quickly can result in greatly reduced comprehension. This means the faster most people read, the less they understand and can make use of.

This isn't a book that will tell you to read as quickly as possible. However, there are a few small improvements you can make to continually tweak the speed of your reading, so what previously took days can now take hours to read and comprehend.

The first tip to increasing your reading speed is to decrease the sub-vocalizations you use.

A sub-vocalization is something you are probably

doing right now. It is when you mentally say and hear the word you are reading. It's a habit that is mostly unnecessary, though is helpful when you want to slow down for increased comprehension. The simple fact is we can understand and process a word more quickly than we can say or hear it. Putting a stop, or at least decreasing, your internal dialogue while reading will greatly help your reading speed. If reading out loud is the first and slowest level, hearing sub-vocalizations is only the second and slightly faster level.

The second tip to reading fast is to practice reading more than one word at a time. Reading word by word is slow and fairly ineffective and can result in incorrect comprehension because you focus on the individual word and not the contextual phrasing or meaning in the text. It's the classic case of getting bogged down in the trees and not being able to see the overall forest.

Start with reading two words together at once. This will require practice, but when you start doing it, you will realize that you can absolutely don't need to read each word individually. You can think of the two words as a contraction. When you get comfortable with two words at once, you can move onto three and four words, until you can look at a sentence that is ten words and reduce it to the two five-word phrases it contains. That's the end goal: to be able to synthesize phrases like you would individual words. One of the keys to reading more at once is to make sure that your

eyes are widened and dilated as if you are trying to use your peripheral vision.

The third tip on speed reading is to improve your visual focus. We constantly lose our place and re-read phrases, and even entire paragraphs, because we get distracted with what's happening elsewhere. This causes you to regress or digress in your reading, which is doubly detrimental to your reading speed. It causes you to have to get back into, "What was this part about, again?"

The simple way to improve your visual focus when reading is to use a placeholder or pointer, such as an index card, pencil, or even your finger. Give your eyes a bulletproof guideline on where to be and where to flow, and they will follow. It will keep you on pace, and prevent reading regression to keep you more immersed in the subject matter.

As I mentioned, this isn't a chapter about speed reading. There are entire books about the subject and I don't want to do it a disservice. It's a chapter about better and more effective reading, and that's where we will move next.

Efficient Reading

This technique applies mostly to books, but also to longer articles and even blog posts.

The underlying idea is most of these books and articles tend to only have one or two big, relevant ideas, tops. Obviously this differs between topics, but there is generally a good reason most of these sources have a "conclusion" section which summarizes all of their findings.

The rest is usually case studies, anecdotes, speculation, or digressions. This is especially true with non-fiction books, as they can typically be summed up in one page if not for the multitude of case studies, examples, different ways of restating a single concept, and evidence and proof for the assertion. What do we do with this knowledge?

We can use it to read extremely efficiently. Your job with reading is to find those one or two big, shiny ideas and try to cut out the rest of the clutter. This means you don't actually need to read a book or article from beginning to end. In fact, that would be a mistake and waste of time.

Note this technique works better for longer pieces since you don't generally need to read shorter pieces more efficiently – they're short!

There are three steps to this technique, and I'll illustrate it with a book example.

The first step is to spend three minutes simply skimming the book's front and back covers, the table of contents, and summary of the book. Think of this

as pre-reading the book, and in fact, you just might be able to get everything out of the book in this step. Many books make their big ideas known up front. If you have time, then you might analyze the introduction or first chapter a bit because the big idea might be there, as well.

The second step is to spend roughly seven minutes skimming the book again, but in more depth. This is when you read the two paragraphs of each chapter to find the big ideas of each chapter, and the big pieces of evidence that support the big ideas. If you see a story or anecdote coming, that's a cue to skip ahead because they are usually only for illustration. During this step, you will also make note of sections to read in more detail in the next step.

The third step is to spend twenty minutes reading specific sections of the book in greater detail. You should know the big ideas from the book already, and you are now looking for clarification and what each chapter adds to the big ideas. Review the highlighted portions from the previous step and read them in greater detail. Then, finish this step by synthesizing what you've read and summarize it in five main bullet points, with three bullet points under each – tops.

Some people like to add to the fourth step of reading the first sentence of each paragraph in each chapter, but it is mostly unnecessary to your goal, which is to find the one or two big ideas! At this point, you should

have a very clear idea of what's contained in the book, and it only took you thirty minutes. If you lack clarity about a certain concept, then you know exactly where to read it straight from the source.

Retain More

Retaining more of what you read is easier than people think. The problem is that most people see reading as a fairly passive activity. As in, they can just sit back and read, and somehow the information will stick in their memory banks.

That's not quite how it works, and for better memory retention and comprehension, you need to make reading a proactive task. The best type of reading is when you read with a purpose because that will keep you focused and alert as to the information in front of you.

Reading with a purpose also turns you into an asker of questions, which is paramount. After every chapter, page, or even long paragraph, there are a series of questions you can be asking yourself to make sense of the information, and make more connections in a participatory manner.

For example, you might ask:

- How does this point relate to the chapter or book in general?

- What did I just learn?
- Why does this matter?
- What are the shortcomings of this?
- What is the counter-argument of this?
- What was necessary for this to occur?
- What is a one-sentence summary of what I just read?

If you are able to actively process these thoughts even occasionally throughout your reading, you will retain far more because the information isn't just a set of facts anymore. They have created a series of connections that you have justification and context on. It's the difference between hearing a bunch of musical notes and hearing an orchestra play together. It creates a bigger impact on your memory because they now have meaning to you through the analyzing questions.

One of the best ways to synthesize and retain information better is to try to predict what happens next, or what happens as a consequence of what you've just read. When you can pull enough information together to make an informed guess, it requires a level of thought and understanding that goes far beyond passive reading.

For example, imagine the kind of thought process you would need if you were to do this with a movie.

You would need to think about the hints that were shown, the motivations and thought processes of the characters, what might typically happen in a similar movie, and why the previous scene influenced you. You could probably list all of these things if asked about the movie prediction, which shows that you are engaged and invested. We can do similar things when we learn. You don't have to make a correct or even good prediction, the important part is to think about what you've seen, try to create patterns, and analyze them.

Finally, to retain more when you read, start from the end. Don't read backwards, but read and review in a different order than how you initially consumed the information. For a book, start from the final points of the last chapter and work your way to the introduction. For an article or study, work your way from the conclusion back to the introduction. What's the point of this?

When you continually read something in the same order, you're creating tread marks in the mud. In other words, you are solidifying information, but only in that specific order and context. You might only retain and remember something if you read or remember what was immediately before or after it.

It's similar to listening to a song playlist in the same order, over and over. Eventually it all melds into one long song, and you can remember and predict the next song based on the current song. But, out of that order

and context, you might not be able to remember or think of it.

When you read out of order and generally approach information from different contexts and angles, you dramatically increase the retention rate, because it's suddenly a three-dimensional picture instead of a flat set of facts.

5

The Art of Taking Great Notes

TAKING NOTES is not just writing down what you heard or read for later consumption.

It's how ideas plant themselves in your head and become part of your memory banks. The proper usage of notes allows ideas to plan themselves in your head and become concrete parts of your memory banks.

Notes are where your learning should always begin, and I don't mean reading other people's notes. When you consume information with the intent to learn, creating your own set of notes to review later is the first step that allows you to synthesize information in any meaningful sort of way.

There are a few different methods that you've probably tried over the years, including outlines, mind

maps, and simply writing down every seemingly big point that you hear or read. Some of these might work for you, but there are almost certainly better ways to organize and intake information. Feel free to take notes on taking notes.

There are four main stages of effective and great notes. They are:

- Note taking
- Note editing
- Note analysis
- Note reflection

Many of us may never make it to the fourth stage, and many of us may not even make it past the second. But that goes to show how much more we could all get from our notes.

The first stage of note taking is where you are just trying to capture all of the big concepts and details. You take them down however you can, and paraphrase arguments and details to support each big concept. Leave space after each section so you can add in additional detail later, and use bullet points and lists wherever possible. Make sure to note areas where clarification and later research is required.

It's best to take this initial set of notes by hand. You have to spend more time on each word you write, and

you also have to be more selective with what you write, because you can't possibly write everything. It forces you to edit the information you are recording at the outset. Then, for the next stages, you can transfer your handwritten notes to any other medium – but the initial stage is always best by hand.

In the same vein, don't rely on transcriptions of full-out recordings of the information that you need. Always insist on taking your own notes so you can immediately summarize and analyze the important information.

The next stage is note editing, and this is the stage where you go back over your initial set of notes and thoroughly edit what you've written, go over everything and write it all out again. This helps comprehension and to find blind spots of knowledge.

Conduct additional research wherever necessary, and collect and organize your notes to fit together with everything else you have on the topic. Review more complex concepts and summarize them, highlight areas that need special emphasis, and make sure that you know where to find any information for easy reference.

The second stage is where you make your notes easy to understand and read for someone to pick up out of the blue without any prior knowledge on the topic. Remember, you are not designing your notes for the expert that is deep in the midst of studying. You are designing them to battle your fading memory, so you

need to leave contextual clues and information to help yourself. It's also a good idea to leave references to page numbers, books, and articles in your notes where you can easily research for original source information.

The third stage is one that you may not have reached lately. The third stage is note analysis, and it's when you actively summarize each section and try to boil everything down to as short a snippet as possible. This is where you use memory techniques such as acrostics and mnemonics.

It's also where you attempt to connect each concept to the other, either as a consequence or by noting how they are related. The general idea of this stage is to gain a deeper understanding of your notes beyond a shallow recitation of facts. To do that, you can ask yourself how concepts fit together and why they were even mentioned in the same section. Ask how they help further your understanding and overarching goal for learning in the first place.

The final stage is note reflection. This usually involves discussion of your notes with other people to make sure that everything you understand is correct, and to create a further level of understanding by open discussion and group analysis. After all, two heads are better than one, and two perspectives are better than one. This can be a peer, or even a teacher or professor.

Focus not on the facts but on the analysis, summaries, and conceptual understanding that you reached in the

third stage. They are what matter in the grand scheme of the topic, and they are what will allow you to make judgment calls in unfamiliar situations.

It's helpful to know facts about Spanish history, but it's far more helpful to understand the role of religion and imperialism, because that will allow you to understand the ecosystem of the day, and why the events occurred in that way. Seek feedback and —this is important— actively try to find gaps of knowledge or where you might be wrong. Attempt to poke holes in your notes and knowledge, which will allow you to reinforce what you're correct about.

The general trend is to not take notes passively, and understand that your task has only begun after you've taken them from your initial consumption of information. Each time you review, you also have to make an effort to make it as participatory as possible so you don't end up just skimming your beautiful notes passively and lazily.

When you review, give yourself a specific task as opposed to just "reviewing your notes." A specific task would be something like organizing specific concepts, looking for connections between other concepts, ordering the importance of the supporting arguments to bigger concepts, or making a map of the concepts and seeing how they connect visually.

The most famous method of note taking is called the Cornell method, and it actually encompasses much of

the aforementioned four stages of great notes. Here's how it works.

On your handwritten sheet for note taking, split it down the middle and into two columns. Label the right column "Notes" and label the left column "Cues." Leave a couple of inches empty at the bottom of the page and label that section "Summary."

You now have three distinct sections, but you will only be taking notes in the Notes section. This is where you take normal notes on the bigger concepts with supporting detail as concisely as possible. Make sure to skip some space between points so you can fill in more detail and clarification at a later point. Draw charts and diagrams and make lists where appropriate, and give your best effort to capturing what matters. You don't need to think about organization or highlighting while you are taking the initial notes. Just write what you hear or read, and give as complete a picture as possible.

After you're done taking notes, move on to the left Cues side. This is where for each section or concept, you filter and analyze the Notes side and write the important parts on the Cues side. Where the Notes side is more of a jumbled mess, the Cues side is a relatively organized account of the topic at hand – basically the same information is on each side. Write the main supporting facts and anything that matters, but in a more organized way. There is the added benefit of having to go through your notes immediately

and synthesizing everything and drawing out what's important and what's not.

Finally, after you're done with the Notes and Cues sides, move to the Summary section at the bottom. This is where you attempt to summarize everything you've just taken notes on into a few top-level ideas and statements, with only the important supporting facts or exceptions to the rules. You want to say as much in as few words as possible, the reason being that when you review your notes, you want to be able to understand quickly and not have to deconstruct and analyze all over again. You want to be able to skim the Summary and Cues section and move on.

There are similarities between the Cornell Method and the four stages of note taking, but in each case, you have created your own study guide. Better yet, you also have the entire process you used to create it documented on the same page, from original notes to synthesis and summarization. You have a record of information that allows you to go as deep as you want, or refer to whatever you want.

Overall, taking notes is not a lazy, passive activity. That's the real secret of great notes. They are intended to serve as something you can refer to, instantly understand, and be helpful, as opposed to having to decipher them. This takes work and usually won't occur on the first pass through.

6

Best Practices for Practicing

WHAT IS the instant way to become an expert at something after learning about it?

Practicing it! Much to the chagrin of children sitting angrily at their pianos across the world, practice is indeed the only way you will improve and rise to a level of expertise, even if you have the innate talent of Mozart.

However, just like learning, taking notes, and reading (most of what we have discussed in this book thus far), there are ways we think are beneficial and successful, and there are ways that actually are. In other words, we are most likely not practicing the best way we can, and if we are, we may not be doing it for the correct reasons.

Practice can sometimes be hard to quantify, because

we generally think it refers to just repeating an action or doing something over and over until we feel better about it. While this is true, it's overly vague and doesn't lead to significant expertise because there's no purpose or system behind it.

Before getting to the finer points of practice, deliberate practice, and what really moves the needle in your practice sessions, I want to touch upon some more foundational practice tips you may already be familiar with. Throughout this chapter, I want to use the example of becoming better at playing an instrument: the violin.

The first step is commitment. Not just the commitment to practicing, but the commitment to not simply breeze through it and passively participate and go through the motions. Commit to 100% focus every time you practice. Commit to the knowledge it will be tiring and exhausting, and there is no easy way to actually practice. Getting better at something involves straying outside of your comfort zone. It will involve no small amount of struggle. You will feel uncomfortable and lacking in your abilities when you attempt to climb higher and higher. So, commit to all of this. Violinists must commit to their fingers hurting and being sore, their arms cramping, their eyes hurting from reading notes, and overall frustration from their fingers not doing what they want.

Set the expectation of commitment and that it

will be a challenge for you to overcome, not to be discouraged by.

The second step is similar. You must practice to the edge of your capacities. This means that there is an optimal level of practice difficulty you should aim for. Aiming too high will discourage you, and aiming too low will bore you and not lead to any improvement. You want to find the sweet spot that pushes you to the edge of your current abilities because you will feel encouraging triumph and accomplishment. For the budding violinist, this means to attempt to play and practice pieces that are slightly more difficult than you think you'd be able to play, or even a piece that has some very difficult parts, but is otherwise average in difficulty. Improvement typically doesn't happen in huge leaps (unless you are a beginner) – it happens in small increments. You should tailor your practice to this pattern and keep yourself motivated and realistic.

Third, it's important to keep giving yourself positive feedback surrounding your practice sessions. The nature of practice is naturally depressing since it involves no small amount of failure. When you have too many failures consecutively, you might eventually start to believe that you completely lack the ability and talent for whatever you are practicing.

Focus on what you've achieved and not what you failed at. Focus on where you started and where you currently are. Review and tally up how many hours

you spend weekly or monthly so you can visually understand how much work you put in, and not feel like you're not working at all.

The budding violinist might record themselves on a monthly basis so they can see their improvement, or when they first start to learn a piece versus the point of mastery over it. Sometimes it's only when we see big contrasts do we feel satisfied with the work we put in.

Realize that improvement is never 100% linear, and you won't feel like you clearly improve every session. Sometimes it might feel like you're taking a step back, but in reality, no one can perform 100% of the time. Just imagine how the stock market chart looks. There's a large upward trend, but there might be dips every once in a while.

Fourth, in addition to positive feedback from yourself, seek immediate feedback from others, negative or positive. This is so you don't build bad habits, or build upon incorrect assumptions and actions. You need to be able to correct your course, and addressing the flaw as quickly as possible is what makes the biggest impact before you internalize it. This allows practice to continue correctly into the future.

In fact, spend most of your time on negative feedback. You likely already know what you're good at. The negative feedback will uncover any blind spots you may possess and fix the weakest link of your chain.

If you don't correct yourself, you are teaching yourself to do something wrong. It's a good idea to attempt to solicit feedback from someone who is (1) not naturally talented, and (2) close to your level of expertise because they will be able to give you highly relevant and articulate feedback, because they understand exactly what you are asking and doing.

We started the chapter with general guidelines for better practice, and now it's time to dive deeper into one of the finer points: deliberate practice.

Deliberate practice was a term coined by John Hayes of Carnegie Mellon University. In short, it describes the best way to practice is to break your main goal down into numerous sub-skills that contribute to the goal. Then, instead of rehearsing the main goal, focus on each sub-skill and bring them to the point of proficiency, one at a time.

For example, there are many sub-skills involved if you wish to perform a violin piece at expert proficiency. You must work on finger strength, finger speed, musical emotion and dynamics, performance skills, stage presence, memorization, and watching the conductor, just to name a few. Deliberate practice would be isolating each of those sub-skills and working on them individually for hours until they become a relative strength.

When you are able to do this for each sub-skill, it

can be said that you have fewer weaknesses, and your overall performance level will rise substantially.

Deliberate practice is the art of mastering smaller skills that contribute to your overall goal. A skill is only as strong as it's weakest link, and you are making sure that you have none. Can a racecar win races if it has a top of the line body and wheels, but engine of a 1980 Honda Civic? There's no hope without paying attention to each contributing component.

The practice of deliberate practice also teaches you to analyze the goal you are working towards, and what is involved in reaching it. You objectively assess what is and is not working and you can more accurately pinpoint your weaknesses and strengths. This is a valuable skill to learn in and of itself, because you are learning to break problems down and solve them.

Here's what deliberate practice looks like in gaining a new skill versus tuning up an existing skill: let's suppose that you want to learn how to lift weights in the gym.

Think about the sub-skills that are involved in lifting weights, then start attacking them one at a time.

You'd start by learning safety rules for each exercise you want to learn. If you wanted to learn fifteen exercises, this could take a while.

Next, you would learn how to do each exercise to

get the most out of it. You'd learn proper form and what to look out for in each of the fifteen exercises. Learning techniques would be a specific sub-skill in itself for each lift.

Then, you would learn how each exercise contributes to your body and how to construct a workout that gives you a balanced physique. People respond differently, so this could take a few sessions in itself.

The contrast is going to a gym and essentially winging it by jumping under a bar and lifting without a clear purpose or understanding of what you're doing. You might even spend hours a week doing this, but unless you understand the proper safety, form, and technique, you won't be fulfilling your gym potential.

Many people think sheer hard work is what will propel them to the top. It's certainly a component, but most people who are working hard are merely developing the skill of hard work, not necessarily playing violin or lifting weights. Deliberate practice is the differentiating factor.

One final wrinkle in the argument for deliberate practice comes in the form of a study from Robert Duke at the University of Texas at Austin, who had pianists learn a complex passage of music, and noted the learning habits of those who performed best at the study's end.

The top strategies became clear.

Identification of problem areas, and subsequent emphasis and focus until the problem was nonexistent. The key for the best pianists was how they handled their problems and weaknesses. They weren't innately better or made fewer mistakes at the outset, they analyzed what they needed to focus on and rehearsed those specifics spots until they were no longer weaknesses. They made sure they didn't continue to make mistakes and learn incorrectly, and correctly identified what needed to happen to improve the piece as a whole.

It sounds remarkably similar to what occurs in deliberate practice.

7

Elephant Memory Techniques

IMPROVING YOUR memory is one of the biggest steps you can take towards being an expert, learning better, and increasing your knowledge.

The term "improving your memory" by itself is actually hazy because we have different types of memory. What most people intend to do is improve their long-term memory, but it's not always what happens.

It's helpful to begin any discussion about memory talking about its components so you can understand how to better achieve your memory goals.

There are three types of memory and they have very different purposes.

1. Sensory memory

2. Short term/working memory
3. Long-term memory

Sensory memory holds both conscious and subconscious information you gain from your five senses. It helps you make sense of your environment and shapes your perception. However, you only remember or perceive these things for as long as they are necessary or useful, and that can be only a few seconds. These are mostly things we don't really notice consciously.

Short term, or working memory, is information you consciously remember for short periods of time without rehearsing or actively trying to commit them to memory. For most people, studies have shown this is roughly seven items for up to thirty seconds. In other words, short term memory can hold seven items, but you will likely forget most of them after thirty seconds.

Imagine that you are trying to remember someone's phone number so you can dial it before it leaves your brain. You are relying on your short term memory to hold those numbers, and you can't hold them forever, so you need to rush to dial the number as quickly as possible. The same feeling occurs when we try to remember license plate numbers and shopping lists.

We instinctively repeat and rehearse the items to ourselves to try to push them into the final phase of memory: long-term memory.

Long-term memory is typically the end goal for whatever we try to memorize or learn. Long-term memory is essentially unlimited and forever, subject to how important the information is and how much it was rehearsed.

There are three steps that push information into memory: encoding, storage, and retrieval.

Encoding is when information is consumed and the brain links the new information to something familiar to make it meaningful and make it stay. Storage is when memories are retained, typically by practice or rehearsal of some sort. Retrieval is when you pluck the memory out of your memory banks and access it to use it in some way.

Short-term memory and long-term memory are stored in different parts of the brain. Short-term memory resides in the frontal lobe of the cerebral cortex, but information stored in long-term memory is first held in the hippocampus, then transferred to the cerebral cortex for permanent storage.

These are important because most of the reasons we forget are related to one of these steps of memory creation. For example, forgetting something in your short-term memory is a result of insufficient encoding, while forgetting something from your long-term memory is a result of faulty retrieval. This has been dubbed the forgetting curve by scientist Hermann Ebbinghaus.

Ebbinghaus posited that memories will fade or not be retained if there is insufficient rehearsal and practice. He estimated that people typically remember only 50% of newly learned information three weeks after exposure, and they remember only 10% eight weeks after exposure. Additional studies have confirmed that it's possible to retain up to 80% of newly learned information if you review and rehearse it within twenty-four hours after exposure.

Our brains are always trying to make sense of the world through limited means. Our memory is selective and wants to filter out the useless chatter we experience on a daily basis. If you rehearse something and repeatedly expose yourself to it soon thereafter, it's a signal to your brain that this information shouldn't be filtered, and actually deserves some mental bandwidth.

In other words, if you learn something on Wednesday, the first time you should review it is later that night, and then every day after. Use it or lose it.

This is the basis for the technique generally accepted as most powerful and effective in increasing your memory: spaced repetition.

Spaced Repetition

Spaced repetition is just what it sounds like. In order to commit more to memory and retain information better,

space out your rehearsal and exposure to it over as long a period as possible. In other words, you will remember something far better if you study it for one hour a day, versus twenty hours in one weekend. This goes for just about everything you could possibly learn. Additional research has shown that seeing something twenty times in one day is far less effective than seeing something ten times over the course of seven days.

Spaced repetition makes more sense if you imagine your brain as a muscle. Muscles can't be exercised all the time, and then put back to work with little to no recovery. Your brain needs time to make connections between concepts, create muscle memory, and generally become familiar with something. Sleep has been shown to be where neural connections are made, and it's not just mental. Synaptic connections are made in your brain and dendrites are stimulated.

Here's a look at what a schedule focused on spaced repetition might look like.

Monday at 10:00 AM – learn initial facts about Spanish history. You accumulate five pages of notes.

Monday at 8:00 PM – review notes about Spanish history, but don't just review passively. Make sure to try to recall the information from your own memory. Recalling is a much better way to processing information than simply re-reading and reviewing. This might only take twenty minutes.

Tuesday at 10:00 AM – try to recall the information without looking at your notes much. After you first try to actively recall as much as possible, go back through your notes to see what you missed and make note of what you need to pay closer attention to. This will probably take only fifteen minutes.

Tuesday at 8:00 PM – review notes. This will take ten minutes.

Wednesday at 4:00 PM – try to independently recall the information again, and only look at your notes once you are done to see what else you have missed. This will take only ten minutes. Make sure not to skip any steps.

Thursday at 6:00 PM – review notes. This will take ten minutes.

Friday at 10:00 AM – active recall session. This will take ten minutes.

Looking at this schedule, note that you are only studying an additional 75 minutes throughout the week, but you've managed to go through the entire lesson a whopping six additional times. Not only that, you've likely committed most of it to memory because you are using active recall instead of passively reviewing your notes.

You're ready for a test the next Monday. Actually, you're ready for a test by Friday afternoon. Spaced

repetition gives your brain time to process concepts and make it's own connections and leaps because of the repetition.

Think about what happens when you have repeated exposure to a concept. The first couple of exposures you may not see anything new. As you get more familiar with it and stop going through the motions, you begin to examine it on a deeper level and think about the context surrounding it. You begin to relate it to other concepts or information, and you generally make sense of it below surface level.

All of this, of course, is designed to push information from your short-term memory into your long-term memory. That's why cramming, or studying at the last minute, isn't an effective means of learning. Very little tends to make it into long-term memory because of the lack of repetition and deeper analysis.

Just as an illustration of the applicability of spaced repetition, Paul Pimsleur discovered that for his audio-based language learning program, there were very specific pauses that led to increased learning. In other words, there were very specific intervals of time between the repetitions that showed better language learning and retention.

The intervals he discovered were: 5 seconds, 25 seconds, 2 minutes, 10 minutes, 1 hour, 5 hours, 1 day, 5 days, 25 days, 4 months, and 2 years. This shows the

importance of repetition, especially soon after initial exposure.

Memories are much better created when they are processed and analyzed on a deeper level, because they form a vivid mental image versus a set of facts and descriptions that the brain filters as boring and useless.

Flashcards

Flashcards are one of the best ways to memorize information. They force recall, and they aren't passive. You must actively recall and state what is on the other side of the flashcard, and it's this act of accessing a potential memory that cements its status.

In order to make best use of your flashcards, commit to making two sets. The first set will contain mere definitions and single concepts. One word prompts for one word or sentence answers.

The second set of flashcards will contain as much information about a single concept as possible, so you will be forced to recall all of that with the prompt of a single word. This is also known as chunking information, where it's advantageous to your short-term memory (which can only hold on average seven items) to remember information as a large chunk, rather than as smaller, individual components. This means when you put more information on each flashcard, that set of information becomes one item versus five items.

When you go through your flashcards, put the cards you got wrong back into the middle or front of your stack so you will see them sooner and more frequently. This helps you work through your mistakes and commit them to memory more quickly.

Overall, you are familiar with flashcards and have likely used them, so there isn't much for me to add here that would teach you something new. Just make sure to understand flashcards aren't a passive activity. You need to actively recall the other side of the flashcard, recite it out loud, then strive to recall more from that single prompt.

Mnemonics

A mnemonic device is most commonly seen as an acronym, where the first letter might represent a word for each. You can make mnemonics for just about anything.

For example, the colors of the rainbow are far more easily remembered as ROY G BIV (red, orange, yellow, green, blue, indigo, violet).

Not much more clarification is necessary here, other than to note that while acronyms are the most common, you can create phrases as mnemonics as well. The point is to give meaning to something that you can more easily remember, and this can be different for everyone. Here are a couple more examples:

The classification system for organisms is far more easily remembered as Devoted(or some other D-word) King Philip Came Over For Good Soup (domain, kingdom, phylum, class, order, family, genus, species).

The order of the planets of our solar system: My Very Easy Method: Just Say Understand Now (Mercury, Venus, Earth, Mars, Jupiter, Saturn, Uranus, Neptune).

The list goes on. The more vivid and outlandish the acronym or imagery, the better and easier to remember.

Stories

Creating stories, or using metaphors and analogies function on the same principle as mnemonics. They substitute a series of information that is difficult to remember with something simpler to remember that has personal meaning to you.

Here's a simple example of something that I've remembered for the past twelve years because of how it illustrated information so perfectly in my mind. Humans have two types of receptors in their eyes, rods and cones. One is for perceiving black and white, and the other is for perceiving color. Which is which?

Well, traffic cones are bright orange, while rods resemble the silver poles that hold up stop signs. Therefore, cones perceive color, and rods perceive black and white.

What you're doing is drawing out the main elements of something and putting it into something you understand and remember. Put it into a context that is so obvious to you that all you have to do is be prompted.

Find something with one or two striking characteristics, and think about how it can relate to Spanish history and say, "It's similar to the Inquisition because..." If a story has a good guy and a bad guy, you can characterize them as the historical figures. You can think about them in terms of the difference between motorcycles and cars. A particular aspect might seem like the process of baking a cake. The end result may remind someone of how your mother treated you when you refused to come home for Christmas that one year.

A picture of a tree might remind you of the geography of a country because of the curves of the branches.

You can use players on your favorite baseball team to memorize the members of a country's government. Who resembles whom and why? You can use a song to remind you of a history lesson because the song is about rebuilding.

It's also this active analysis and application of a story, imagery, or metaphor to your information that further helps memory become solidified. You're searching to tie new information into existing

information in an engaging manner. You might even remember the thought process more than the story or metaphor itself.

8

Make Learning Secondary

"THAT IS the way to learn the most, that when you are doing something with such enjoyment that you don't notice that the time passes." – Albert Einstein to his son, Hans Einstein

There is a lot of wisdom to unpack in that simple sentence Einstein once uttered to his son, and it ties in directly with the focus of this chapter.

It's a straightforward premise. If you are lucky enough to be consumed with a goal or objective, and achieving that goal or objective happens to require the acquisition of skills or knowledge, then you won't even notice. Your learning and expertise become second nature, all in pursuit of that goal.

I want to briefly repeat the story I told in the introduction of this book. I had a very motivating goal of talking to a girl in my Spanish class, Jessica. She

tended to turn around and ask me for help because she was perhaps the one person who paid less attention than me in class, so I vowed to get better at Spanish so she would continue talking to me.

In this pursuit for her attention, I studied Spanish like a madman, and even researched obscure references and vocabulary to impress her. I didn't know it at the time, but I had made learning secondary, and the pursuit of my goal was my biggest priority.

I learned as a byproduct, and that is perhaps the easiest way of all to learn.

Here's another example which involves my older sibling. When he was growing up, the Internet was just starting to become popular. Of course, with the Internet came chat rooms, message boards, and all sorts of communication with people that weren't right next to you. It opened the world up for many people. I remember watching him sit at the family computer struggling to type.

One day he downloaded some sort of chat program, which I now realized was AOL Instant Messenger – the infamous AIM that nearly every adolescent, teenager, and young adult used at the time. It couldn't have been one or two weeks later that I walked past him at the computer again, and couldn't help but notice how noisy and busy the keyboard was. His typing speed had probably quadrupled in just that week since

downloading AIM. He became nearly obsessed with chatting online, and that obsession translated into competency quite quickly.

He had made learning how to type secondary in pursuit of his primary goal of talking to his friends online more quickly! All he wanted to do was type faster so he could tell jokes with proper timing and not get beat to the punch line by his friends, and he found a way to get that done through typing more quickly. His accuracy and so-called technique would probably have been better if he attended typing classes, but he was an incredibly fast typist, with all credit going to AIM.

Here's a final example to illustrate that making learning second can lead you to learning and knowledge without you even realizing it.

This story is about one of my friends from college. When he was still living in the dorms, he was surrounded by people who happened to play the guitar. They had all learned at some point when they were teenagers, and brought their guitars to college to serenade women. Occasionally, they also lugged all of their guitars into the same room and jammed out to classic rock songs as a band.

Feeling left out, my friend asked if he could use one of their roommates' guitars when they weren't there. It wasn't a problem, so my friend began learning how to play guitar on his own, practicing the songs his

dorm mates jammed to. It wasn't that he felt left out of wanted to fit in, he just saw music as a fun group activity and wanted to be able to participate.

The next time the group gathered to jam, he was able to join in on the fun, and when they went through various songs in their repertoire, he was able to learn on the fly and play quietly in the background before becoming more confident and playing more loudly. He started to bond with these guys, and learned more and better guitar so the group could play more complex tunes and solos.

He is another shining example of why, if possible, you should make learning secondary.

Given the proper motivation, you can make it so learning and knowledge isn't a chore, and is rather a rung on the ladder to your overall goal and sense of gratification. What's more important when you have a bigger goal is that you focus on efficiently making something work. You might not be worried about the specifics as much, but you will probably have the same end result. From there, you have the choice to start deliberate practice, rehearsal, and fine-tuning everything, but simply having the right motivation this will get you to a point of competency and even make you stand out.

Skill, expertise, and learning can all come as a byproduct of your overall goal. What do we do with this knowledge?

Understand that a motivation other than learning and knowledge is your most powerful learning tool. You have to see the forest through the trees and understand the rewards and benefits of what your actions are leading towards. In essence, everything you learn, or want to become better at, is a tool on the way to your overarching goal or project.

Don't have a goal or project? Make one that will make the acquisition of a desired skill necessary, but not the primary focus. For instance, if you want to learn better geography, start playing board games that require such knowledge. If you want to get better at skiing, start entering small, local competitions which will force you to improve. If you want to get better a typing, play a game that requires quick and accurate typing. If you want to learn a language more quickly, watch television shows that require greater vocabulary.

Make learning the journey, not the end point.

It's important to mention that it's not wise to always rely on motivation or inspiration. Those require you to be in a positive state of mind, which isn't always possible. It also puts you in a mindset where you have a prerequisite to learning and focusing. You need to feel inspired, you need to feel motivated, or you need to be in the right state of mind. This, we all know, definitely isn't always possible.

That's why I want to touch upon what I call the 10-Minute Rule. It works in two ways. First, if you

don't feel like doing something, just do it for ten minutes, then you can stop. Of course, you'll rarely stop at the ten-minute mark because you'll have built up momentum and destroyed what was keeping you lazy: inertia.

Second, whenever you feel like stopping a task or quitting for the day, just give it ten more minutes until you stop. You may not continue much past this, but giving yourself a specific deadline will make you want to finish as much as possible in that time, and it will make you just a tad bit more productive. Your motivation may be waning, but your discipline will keep you working.

The other big lesson of this chapter is that doing, using, and applying is the most important part of learning, hands down. Recall the pyramid of learning where the most passive methods of learning yielded the least memory retention. When you do, use, and apply your knowledge, you are at the bottom of the pyramid which is participatory and active. It's more work to be sure, and most of us like to slide down the path of least resistance.

Doing and getting your hands dirty allows you to find patterns and make connections that observation and study would never show you. I'd go so far as to say you will never master anything without some firsthand experience. Dan Coyle, talent researcher and scientist, suggested that the rule of two-thirds is most effective

when learning or acquiring a new skill. You should spend one third of the time reading and researching, and the other two thirds actually doing and practicing.

You can only learn so much about playing the guitar by watching videos and reading tutorials. Don't expect to be able to play like Jimi Hendrix the first time you pick the guitar up if you don't practice and do. If you're a complete neophyte, then you need to start with research and bone up on the ground rules and boundaries. Then, go and do.

Knowledge from research by itself is useless without the experience to back it up. When you combine those two, you gain intuition and judgment, which is usually the true goal.

9

How to CRAM

HOWEVER MANY warnings or pieces of advice that advocate spaced repetition, or the notion to begin studying and learning ahead of time, many of us still won't.

That's for good reason. We get busy with other things and can't break our stride to review something even for five minutes. We have many other subjects to learn and study. We just feel lazy and tired at the end of a long day. These are all legitimate excuses.

We know this isn't the most effective way to learn, but unfortunately it's what we're stuck with sometimes. There's a saving grace – recall that most effective learning targets long-term memory. That's the main goal of spaced repetition, to make the leap from short-term memory to long-term memory, where you no longer have to rehearse or practice it to remember it.

You can simply recall it with a bit of thought and it's in your brain for an indefinite period of time.

To cram for a test, exam, or other type of evaluation, we don't need material to make it to our long-term memory. We just need it to make it slightly past our working memory and be partially encoded into our long-term memory. We don't need to be able to recall anything the day after, so it's like we only need something to stick for a few hours.

This chapter optimizes for learning as much as possible in as little time as possible, while also ensuring that you can retain it. It's a difficult task, but if you're going to pull an all-nighter, you might as well do it in the right way.

Chunking

I discussed chunking briefly in the previous chapter, but it's more appropriate to discuss it in detail here. Chunking is the act of turning five pieces of information into one piece of information for the sake of memorization.

For example, which is easier to memorize: 3 3 5 9 1 0 or 33 59 10? That's how chunking works. You do it every time you try to keep an account or telephone number in your memory before you use it. You simply combine information on a conceptual or semantic level such that your memory has to hold fewer objects.

Recall that our short-term memories can only hold seven items on the top range. Chunking gets around this because where there was once six numbers to remember, now there are three. That's a type of chunking that is called grouping. You create something to memorize from seemingly unrelated and random pieces of information. Here are a couple more examples to illustrate how to use chunking to your advantage.

If you have a list of things to purchase, you can create a mnemonic device, like mentioned previously, where the first letter of each item forms a new word. If you want to buy pears, apples, bananas, and underwear, that forms the word PABU, which is easier to remember or write down.

For the same list of things to purchase, you can also just push the words together. If you want pears, apples, bananas, and underwear, you could try to remember the word "pe-ap-ba-un," which represents all of the information on the list. You're substituting four pieces of information for one.

Another example is to visualize a scene or environment where all the elements work together. See a picture mentally of a setting that contains all of the aforementioned items, and keep in mind there are four of them total. Where might you see three pieces of fruit and a pair of underwear? Perhaps a hoarder's kitchen table, or an obscene grocery store. The more vivid the setting, the more memorable it will be.

In each of these cases, you're creating something new, or referring to something already in your memory that reminds you of multiple pieces of information. Make a connection and create something meaningful, which is easier to remember. This is the reason raw data and information rarely ever makes it to long-term memory. The moment you can see a pattern form, it is easier to remember.

Pomodoro Technique

The Pomodoro Technique is a focus technique that promotes undistracted work and planned breaks. It's straightforward. You look at your study time in thirty-minute blocks. You will focus, turn off your phone, and ignore all distractions for twenty-five minutes, and then take a planned break for only five minutes to give your brain a break to not run at full capacity. This is one block, and immediately after, you dive into another thirty-minute block.

Most practitioners of the Pomodoro Technique make it their goal to complete eight thirty-minute blocks, but you might find that difficult if you're new to the concept. My recommendation is to aim for three blocks at first, and see how you feel at that point.

The greater purpose of the Pomodoro Technique is to avoid multitasking, and wasting mental capital switching between tasks and backtracking, while you

try to find where you were. This frequently will result in one step forward, and one step backward, and after a couple of hours, you might find that you've only made minimal progress across all your tasks. Complete attention and focus for twenty-five minutes, no small amount of time, will allow you to build momentum and really make way through your information.

What's more, it's pretty likely that you'll overshoot twenty-five minutes, in which case, you should take a ten-minute break after fifty minutes. There is absolutely something to be said for putting your head down and grinding for a bit.

The Pomodoro Technique also brings awareness to your need for breaks and distractions. It's natural that we can't sustain focus all the time. You can't sprint endlessly, you would need a break eventually before you burn out. Sometimes your mind is fried and full, such as when you start reading the same page over and over without really comprehending it. That's when you know you need a break. It's a natural part of the memorization and learning process, even when you are cramming.

Continually Summarize

Remember, there's limited time and limited space in your memory banks when you're cramming, so you need to consume and memorize as little information as

possible that will impart as much meaning as possible.

The goal is to give meaning and association to smaller pieces of information. Essentially, you want to be able to cram a paragraph's worth of information and recall into a single sentence. The way to do this is to re-write and re-summarize your notes into shorter and shorter versions, until they can ideally all fit onto a single piece of paper (or even an index card, depending on the context). Ideally you also write this all by hand, because you are forced to be economical with your words when writing by hand.

Let's say you start with ten pages of notes, which you first summarize and condense into three pages. This will force you to analyze what's important and filter all the clutter in your subject matter. You'll also begin memorizing on a deeper level when you review your material with this type of goal.

Then, you summarize the three pages into one page. The act of combing through your material and thinking, "Is this important and does this contribute to the overall point?" is just as important as the actual act of writing out the new summary version.

Finally, you might summarize your single page so it fits onto an index card, which will further force you to condense, filter, and analyze the important parts. By this point, you've essentially written your notes three additional times, but in a way that is friendly to your

limited memory banks at the moment. What's more, it's not like you will only remember what is only on the index card. Each sentence and bullet point will have so much more meaning and information behind it because you've filtered it three times and thought about it deeply.

You're working with limited space, and continually summarizing your material is going to make the most of it.

Make Connections

Raw information on the page isn't going to make it to your memory very easily. What you must do is give meaning to it, make it relate to information you already know, and simply make it memory-worthy.

First, make sure you understand your material. When you comprehend something, it will be easier to cram into your brain than something that is a puzzle to you.

Second, actively seek to make as many connections to existing knowledge as possible by continually asking, "It's like X, except Y..." It doesn't matter if it's not particularly related, just make a connection as to how they might relate. It's this deeper analysis that hardcodes information, not the actual analogy, metaphor, or comparison. Additional questions to ask to make connections to existing information are, "It's

the opposite of X…" and "This has the following three elements in common with X…"

Third, reason out loud to yourself. This is where you use phrases such as, "So this X happened because Y…" and "Z only occurred because X…" You're basically narrating how everything fits together. Understanding context and logical flow will help your memorization.

Use Space

You might not be able to do true spaced repetition if you are cramming at the last minute, but you can emulate it in a small way. Instead of studying subject X for three hours only at night, seek to study it one hour each three times a day, with a few hours between each exposure.

Recall that memories need time to be encoded and stick in the brain. You are doing the best imitation of spaced repetition you can with what you have available. To get the most out of your limited studying time, study something as soon as you wake up, review it at noon, at 4:00 p.m., then 9:00 p.m. – or similar. The point is to review throughout the day and get as much repetition as possible.

During the course of your repetition, make sure to study your notes out of order in order to see them in different contexts, encode better, and also use active recall versus passive reading.

Finally, make sure that you're reciting and rehearsing new information up to the last minute before your test. Your short-term memory can hold seven items on its best day, so you might just save yourself with a piece of information that was never going to fit into your longer term memory. It's like you're juggling. It's inevitable that you drop everything, but it could just so happen that you're juggling something you can use.

10

Learning by Science

THOUGH THERE have been studies interspersed throughout this book, much of it has been to buttress well-known truths about studying and other tips that generally wouldn't surprise you.

This chapter is a little bit different. It is dedicated to the science of learning – specifically, the unexpected conclusions science has yielded about learning that will likely surprise you. As an author, one of the complaints I hear most is that most studies don't really shed light on anything new, and they just confirm what we already know and do instinctually. Hopefully this chapter is a departure and gives you unconventional tips to increase your learning potential, and absorb knowledge like a human sponge.

Exercise Boosts Your Brain

This first scientific study might be less of a surprise than the others.

Separate studies by Professors Crook and Ratey have shown exercise to be beneficial for your learning and memorization efforts because of the extra blood, oxygen, and glucose delivered to the brain. The more it gets, the better it performs, unsurprisingly. This means your brain on a daily basis is not functioning at its peak. It's rather functioning in equilibrium and status quo mode in the absence of any dire need. Put another way, it's conserving energy for when you really need it, but exercise allows you to put your brain into this state of mind whenever you want.

Crook even went so far as to assert that cardiovascular health is the most important factor in learning and memory. Beyond delivering more nutrients to the brain through increased blood flow, physical activity also releases neurochemicals that are beneficial in numerous ways. First, brain-derived neurotrophic factor (BDNF) is released, which assists the brain in cell growth and learning. Neurotransmitters like serotonin, dopamine, and norepinephrine are also released, all of which increase arousal, attention, and alertness.

Taken together, exercise puts the brain into a state of temporary amazingness where problem solving and information retention are second nature. How long

is this temporary state? A study published in *Brain and Cognition* determined that you have somewhere in the neighborhood of fifty-two minutes of boosted capability, depending on how strenuous your exercise was. To capitalize on this type of brain alertness, you can schedule breaks where you increase your heart rate for every sixty to ninety minutes, because it's likely you are starting to fatigue, get bored, and ineffective at that point.

For best results, make sure that it's actual exercise and not just a walk around the block! A study in *Neurobiology of Learning and Memory* addressed this, and researchers found that people completed a task 20% faster after intense exercise versus calmer exercise. The bigger the physical toll, the more hormones and neurotransmitters are released to your memory's benefit. Just imagine how alert and aware you suddenly are if you are driving and almost get into an accident. That's the same sort of brain rush.

In another study, researchers discovered people who exercised three times a week over a period of six months, had an increase in the size of their hippocampus, which is the part of the brain that controls learning and memory. Physical exercise literally led to changes in their brain structure that led to increased memory capacity. This lends credence to the saying of healthy body, healthy mind. If you feel like you are mentally dragging, take a break to get your heart rate elevated.

Treat it like a shot of caffeine without the dreaded hangover. Use your breaks to get some exercise and come back refreshed and ready to absorb.

Change Locations

This next study is about the phenomenon that studying the same material in different locations and environments helps memory retention.

A study by Robert Bjork found that information is remembered and encoded into our memory holistically. This means that if you study Spain in an aquarium, your memory will associate the two subconsciously. Your memory will also associate what you wore that day, what you ate, the smells in the aquarium, and what stood out visually in your environment. They'll all be lumped together as far as your memory is concerned, with the specific information you are trying to remember or learn.

This means two things. First, that it is possible to evoke the memory of Spain just by being exposed to the same smells and visual stimuli. If they are part of your overall memory of the information, then they will act to remind you of the rest of it. In other words, if you studied Spain in an aquarium and see a picture of an aquarium, it's entirely possible to remind you of the information you learned about Spain.

Second, if you change locations frequently while

learning and processing the same information, you are strengthening your memory because it will be associated with multiple locations, smells, and generally stimuli to make you remember it. The researchers deemed this increased neural scaffolding. The more stimuli that triggers that memory or information, the more deeply it is encoded in your memory like a growing web.

A 1978 study added support for the finding that the more stimuli present while you are learning, the deeper information is processed in your brain. There were two groups that had two study sessions. One group studied vocabulary in two different rooms, and the other studied vocabulary in the same room twice. The first group showed far better recall.

What does this mean for you?

You should change locations as frequently as possible while learning the same information. If you can't change your scenery completely, change what's on your desk, the music you are listening to – anything that impacts any of your five senses. The more change of stimuli, the more roots the information will take to your brain.

Scientists have found other links between what memories can be associated with. Ruth Propper of Montclair State University found that even muscle contractions, namely a clenched right fist, could be subconsciously associated with information

and memory if done simultaneously. One group of participants clenched a ball with their right fists while performing a memory task, while other groups either had no ball at all, or clenched their left fists.

The first group routinely performed the best. Why does this work? It could be similar to why changing locations increases memory retention, because the more stimuli, the more cues for the information. Propper also posited that clenching the right hand activates the left side of the brain, which is where memory is generally encoded and recalled.

Feynman Technique

This next point isn't quite the result of a study, but is named for Richard Feynman, one of the world's most famous physicists. That's close enough. The Feynman Technique is typically used for speedy and optimal learning. You can use it to figure out concepts for yourself and determine the vital information you lack, as well as explain complex concepts to other people. It has four steps.

Step one: Choose your concept.

The Feynman Technique is very widely applicable, so let's choose one we can use throughout this section: gravity. Suppose that we want to either understand the basics about gravity, or explain it to someone else.

Step two: Write down an explanation of the concept in plain English.

Is this easy or difficult? This is the truly important step because it will show exactly what you do and do not understand about the concept of gravity. Explain it as simply, yet accurately, as you can in a way that someone who knows nothing about the concept would also understand.

Can you do it, or will you resort to saying, "Well, you know… it's gravity!" This step allows you to see your blind spots and where your explanation starts to fall apart. If you can't perform this step, clearly you don't know as much about it as you thought, and you would be terrible at explaining it to someone else.

Step three: Find your blind spots.

If you were unable to come up with a short description of gravity in the previous step, then it's clear you have large gaps in your knowledge. Research gravity and find a way to describe it in a simple way. You might come up with something like, "The force that causes larger objects to attract smaller objects because of their weight and mass."

Being able to analyze information and break it down in a simple way demonstrates knowledge and understanding. If you can't summarize it in one sentence, you still have blind spots you need to learn about.

Step four: Use an analogy.

Finally, create an analogy for the concept. Making analogies between concepts requires an understanding of the main traits and characteristics of each. This step is to demonstrate whether or not you truly understand it on a deeper level, as well as make it easier to explain. You can look at it as the true test of your understanding and whether you still possess blind spots in your knowledge.

For example, gravity is like when you put your foot into a pool and the fallen leaves on the surface are attracted to it because it causes a barely-seen impact. That impact is gravity.

This step also connects new information to old information and lets you piggyback off a working mental model to understand or explain in greater depth. The Feynman Technique is a rapid way to discover what you know versus what you think you know, and allows you to solidify your knowledge base.

Sleep Learning

You've seen those infomercials. "Listen to this tape in your sleep and wake up a genius and be fluent in French!"

Of course, those are 99% fraudulent, but that 1% represents an interesting recent finding. We can learn

some things in our sleep, but there are specific boundaries of this learning. Professor Reber of Northwestern University split pianists into two groups and had them learn a new passage. Then, all the participants took a ninety-minute nap. For one of the groups, the melody was played quietly during sleep for only four minutes, while the other group had complete silence.

The group who had melody while they were sleeping ended up playing the melody 4% better and more accurately than the other group. That's quite a big difference for only four minutes of apparent sleep learning. Brain scans confirmed that there was increased activity while the melody was played, even during sleep, signaling memory processing.

It's a fairly significant discovery, but can you really just play a recording while you sleep? Not quite. Reber went on to clarify, "As long as the memory is tied to a specific type of sound, it looks like the sound can re-activate and strengthen the previously learned information. It is possible this effect would help with strengthening memories from a classroom or lecture and that it could even help speed up second-language learning."

What does this mean for you? Well, you probably can't learn new information in your sleep, but you can reinforce information you've already learned to some degree, as long as hearing sounds is enough of a cue to trigger your memories and thoughts. For example,

reinforcing a foreign language would work because you could pick up on the distinct sound. You may not be able to decipher specific information, such as the quadratic equation, but you can recall it better if it you associate it with a specific sound.

11

Smart Goals

WE'VE ESTABLISHED that learning has a few different components, from information consumption, memory retention, and actual doing. All of these elements contribute to becoming an expert, but there is a final asp

Creating goals. Why do goals matter in learning?

Human nature prefers the path of least resistance. If you don't construct goals, or at least have an idea of the end point you seek, you won't be properly motivated, and you will likely only do the bare minimum that is required. If you're not trying to accomplish something with your learning or memorizing, then what's the purpose of making an effort at all? What will keep you focused and in check when you have other distractions?

What will keep you from whatever your definition of failure?

If you took a class that never had any tests or exams, would you bother learning or studying? If you put a goal in place, like an exam, then you'd behave very differently with your efforts.

Suffice it to say, goals can assist your learning, and in many cases take it to the next level. There is one method in goal setting that has proven to be heads and shoulders above all others. This is called the SMART method of setting goals, where SMART is actually the acronym S.M.A.R.T.

S.M.A.R.T. stands for Specific, Measurable, Attainable, Relevant, Time-bound. I'll take you through each of these elements separately to see how you can make more effective goals that will help your learning and memory retention.

Specific

Let's suppose you have the goal of losing weight. That by itself isn't a very specific goal. In fact, it's so broad and vague that if you lose even one pound, you could call your goal successful. It doesn't help with planning and preparation, and it certainly doesn't motivate you the way a specific goal would.

A better answer here would take into account

exactly what you want to accomplish, such as, "I want to lose fifteen pounds and fit into the third notch of my brown leather belt."

This makes your goal real because you've placed a number on it and a specific benefit; it's no longer a vague concept. You've put it out there, and now you are capable of failure. This is the reason many of us don't define our goals too clearly. It's the same aversion to a negative reaction that will motivate you and push you to achieve.

You might also be specific as to the entire context behind the goal, which would include:

- Who is involved, if not only yourself.
- When you want to accomplish this goal by.
- Where this goal will occur, if applicable.
- Why you want to accomplish this goal.

The last point is the most important because it solidifies a clear benefit and desire from for reaching this goal. It gives you the long-term view of how your life will change, and can keep you focused when you are stuck or feeling despair. A clear "why" will power you and provide an energy boost because you aren't just starving yourself or eating broccoli, you are doing it for self-esteem, to fit into your pants, and to attract the opposite sex better. This is something you should

articulate at the very beginning, because it shapes everything else.

Measurable

You need a mechanism for determining whether you are getting closer to your overall goal. You have to be able to tell whether there is incremental progress, and if there is a difference from your starting point.

With weight loss, this is straightforward. You only need to step on a scale to see if you are making progress towards your goal weight. For other goals, you need a similarly objective method to measure your progress and how far you've come.

This serves two main purposes. First, seeing progress is incredibly motivating and provides positive feedback. It shows your efforts have payoff, and your actions can directly affect your fate. The subtext is that it motivates you to try harder because thus far, there has been a direct causation from your actions to your goal. That's nice.

Second, measuring your progress keeps you accountable and on track. You can't rely on subjective judgment because you will probably default to the path of least resistance, or be able to otherwise rationalize your poor progress or performance. An objective measure like a scale will never lie to you, and it will never swallow your lies. It will just tell you if what's happening is or isn't good enough.

Attainable

When you set your goals, they must be something that is clearly possible at some point in time by you.

There is a fine line between shooting too low and too high. It can't be overly ambitious, because when you fail to adhere to that trajectory, you may become demotivated. If you shoot too low, then you aren't gaining much.

It's also important to consider what's involved in attaining your goal. A good goal is not something that *could possibly* happen in the future if other circumstances align. It's something that, if you are pushed out of your comfort zone a bit and control what you can control, has an extremely high likelihood of materializing.

When you set the initial goal, factor out everything out of your control. What can you plausibly control and manipulate to your advantage? That directly influences what is attainable, but make sure that you aren't shooting too low to compensate for what is out of your control.

You also need to think about the changes required to achieve your goal, both in your environment and your personality towards things. What would it take to completely change your environment, and what skills or tools would you need to attain to achieve your goal? Take inventory of yourself. If you want to lose

weight, and you are surrounded by friends who all eat terrible fast food every day, and you don't possess a gym membership, what steps are necessary to change your environment and personality?

This keeps you accountable because you won't be able to blame anything external – you have sole responsibility for whether or not you attain your goal.

Relevance

What is the relevance of this goal to your life, overall goals, and happiness? Why does it matter and why do you want to achieve it?

This is similar to the "why" we discussed earlier. You need a compelling "why" because it's what will keep you motivated and on target through the struggle of reaching your goal. Often, we may have trouble articulating these because they are tied to improving our emotional states, i.e. "I want to lose weight because I feel embarrassed and lack confidence."

If you lack an overarching goal or emotional motivation, it's incredibly easy to veer off the path to your goal because there's no backlash. You won't feel like you're missing out on anything.

Time-bound

You must be able to impose a deadline for reaching your goal. A goal without a deadline is just a dream

or, at best, a statement of intent. If you don't have a deadline for your goal, you won't have any urgency or reason to take action *today* instead of tomorrow or next week. This is key to actually carrying through.

Anyone can set goals, but if they are ambiguous as to timing, it's probably not intended to succeed.

If you have a longer-term goal, it can also be helpful to set deadlines for milestones throughout the course of the year so you are aware of where you should be at a certain time. This will provide further check-ins to keep you accountable and impart a sense of urgency.

If I want to lose fifteen pounds in the next year, I want to lose five pounds every month, which is 1.25 pounds every week. It provides much more clarity.

Now that we've gone through each element of S.M.A.R.T. goals, let's go through a few examples to see how they differ from "poor", but exceedingly common, types of goals.

Bob says, "My goal is to start a business!" with no further clarification. This goal is so broad that we don't even know what he is referring to, much less how likely it is to succeed.

Let's take Bob through the steps and create a S.M.A.R.T. goal for him.

- Specific: I want to open my own lawnmower store.
- Measurable: You can measure this goal by the

money the business makes: I will make $10,000 in the first six months of opening my business.

- Attainable: This is attainable, but I need to hire a lawyer and accountant, ignore my family for a while, talk to my mentor more, and change my schedule so I can visit stores every weekend.
- Relevant: This store represents my freedom from being an employee and hopefully will eventually fuel my retirement.
- Time-bound: I want to sign the lease on the store itself in the next two months, and start selling products one month after.

Where Bob once started with "My goal is to start a business!" he now has "My goal is to open my own lawnmower store within two months and make $10,000 within the first six months, and work for myself for the rest of my life."

Here's another example: Elaine says, "I want to become famous in my field." What is her S.M.A.R.T. goal?

- Specific: I want to be the most famous tax attorney in my state.
- Measurable: You can measure this goal by how frequently you are asked to be interviewed or speak on tax issues, as well as how much business you have.

- Attainable: This is attainable, I will need to hire a public relations firm, start writing for newspapers and magazines, and network with fellow attorneys that have sway.
- Relevant: If I can become the most famous tax attorney in my state, I will have a never-ending flow of business and I will be able to stop worrying about money.
- Time-bound: I want to accomplish this goal and have four interviews a month by the end of the year.

You can see how many more elements come up when thinking through your goals, and how going through the S.M.A.R.T. process essentially provides a blueprint for what you need to do. Not only do S.M.A.R.T. goals have a higher chance of success, they can tell you exactly what you are looking for.

S.M.A.R.T. isn't the only guideline that will help you with your goals.

First, sometimes it's better to make goals and success about the effort, and not necessarily the achievement. In other words, it can be motivating at the beginning to make a success just doing something versus doing it well. Just getting to the gym and jogging for ten minutes is a success. Aim for that, versus lifting heavy weights for two hours, as might be ideal to some. Effort and consistency is underrated in goal completion, so make sure to reward it.

Second, your willpower to achieve your goal has limits. Think of it as a battery pack that runs down at the end of the day. This means you should preemptively avoid temptations and distractions, and make it as easy as possible for you to work on your goal. For a weight loss goal, this would mean making it easy to eat healthy and workout by packing your lunch, and always having clean gym clothes, and avoiding buying snacks altogether.

Third, make sure the goals you set are because you want them. Don't set goals that are from other people, or ones that you are bound to by a sense of duty or obligation. You're not going to have a very compelling "why" to motivate yourself to achieve them, and they might be a waste of your precious time. The more a goal is for someone else's expectations, the more of a chore it will feel like.

Finally, don't forget to review and monitor your progress, starting from day one. Often, we are completely blind to incremental progress just because we can't notice the difference. Whatever medium is appropriate, record yourself right from the beginning. You can make it visual so you can tangibly see and appreciate the difference. The point is to incorporate encouragement as a result of seeing your progress.

12

The Trio

SADLY, WE have come to our last chapter on learning, but fear not. This last chapter provides some short yet powerful tips to learn and memorize better.

Incubation

Ever wonder why you get so many ideas when you are standing in the shower?

Shelley Carson of Harvard University came up with the answer. It's counterintuitive, but it's because you are distracted by the shower.

Here's what happens when we over-focus and fixate on something. We become bored and burnt out, and start looking at it from only one perspective or path of possibility. We find ourselves unable to think

differently, like we are stuck in the deep tread in the dirt that repeated traffic from a tire creates.

When we disengage and become distracted by something else that is relatively relaxing, such as shampooing your hair in the shower, that's when a period known as incubation begins. Your conscious brain has stopped thinking about the problem, but it's still ticking and processing under the hood. Disconnecting can essentially put the mind into a state of unconscious pondering and connection. Your brain begins to passively approach the problem from other perspectives and paths that were different from what you fixated on consciously.

This subconscious brainstorming session can lead to flashes of insight that only required a simple shift in perspective or angle. What does this information mean for you?

The theory of incubation is an argument for taking regular breaks, especially if you are stuck on one particular problem or solution. It's not a guarantee you will witness a strike of lightning, but you will at the very least come back refreshed and ready to attack it again from different angles.

Breaks are more productive if you can position them as recovery and subconscious processing, as opposed to rest. More time spent staring blankly at your work is not time well spent. In fact, scrolling down your

social media accounts for fifteen minutes might not be such a bad thing – as long as it's to take a break from something you've been stuck on for a while.

Incubation suggests that we learn and process information on both conscious and subconscious levels, and not always simultaneously. In other words, much of the time we are processing information subconsciously while ignoring it consciously, doing another task, or becoming distracted.

It sounds strikingly similar to spaced repetition. This is something we can use to our advantage if we strategically study and learn throughout the day.

In the morning, start tasks A, B, and C. Dedicate time to each of them. Start each task, take notes, and fully dive into each. For example, if you're a writer, your tasks might be three different articles in the morning. Do your initial research, write outlines, and do some initial analysis. Spend an hour on each article. This is your conscious track of thinking and processing, but your subconscious mind will already be thinking about the prior topics.

Then break for lunch, and generally become distracted with low-demand tasks. Your subconscious track of thought is still working and churning. This is when incubation occurs, and often you will have ideas of how to approach each of the articles. It's as if your brain makes connections when you aren't

actively working on them. Make sure to be ready to take notes and record thoughts during this incubation period. You may not have worked the articles, but your subconscious did.

When you get back to writing your articles, you will have increased insight on how to write them courtesy of your subconscious. Numerous studies have shown conscious multi-tasking to be a myth because people typically expend their mental bandwidth switching between tasks and re-orienting themselves. Incubation might be the only case where multi-tasking is relevant because it's done on a subconscious level.

Teaching

Now that you've learned how to learn and memorize effectively, it's healthy to look at the other end of the spectrum to examine what we can do to become better teachers ourselves.

This section encompasses many of the tactics you've used for yourself, but you'll find they may be slightly different when teaching others.

When you are teaching, you want to focus on comprehension over memorization or breadth. Full comprehension is the foundation upon which everything else is built, because it allows you to make predictions, use intuition, and think critically. Flat facts don't give context or provide actual knowledge. Starting

with memorization reduces everything to flat, boring information, while breadth promotes information over context or understanding.

Comprehension can be improved with the Feynman Technique as covered earlier, in conjunction with continually asking for simple explanations and summaries for each aspect of what you are teaching. The longer the explanations are, the less people understand and are trying to talk *around* the concept.

As the teacher, it's a matter of asking the right questions so people will not only focus on the important parts, but they will also make connections and view information in a relatable manner. You must be the one to draw it out of them. For example, you can ask the following questions to drive your points home:

- What was the main point of this concept?
- Can you summarize this?
- Why does this matter?
- How does this relate to the main point?
- How does this concept connect to the next?
- What happened before, and what will happen after?

You can also play devil's advocate to force people to articulate their thought process and reasoning. These all drive concepts deeper than rote memorization or lectures.

Be sure to accommodate for people's learning styles. Remember there is some debate as to whether learning styles are a legitimate differentiation, but also recall that you can see each style as a tool for increased engagement and interest. In fact, evidence throughout the book has shown that using multiple types of media and stimuli are best for retention, because of the increased neural scaffolding that occurs. In other words, the way more information is consumed, the more likely it is to stick and be useful.

Place a premium on repetition throughout the day. As opposed to a three-hour block of intense study on one topic, divide it into one-hour blocks on consecutive days. This requires foresight and smart planning to take advantage of the benefits of spaced repetition. To emphasize repetition, create flashcards and place a requirement of active recall, rather than re-statement and reading. The upside of this more mentally fatiguing manner of study is that you can accomplish more in less time, so the sessions may be much shorter.

People are typically in need of motivation, and you can provide that if you again ask your students the right questions. Just like you need your compelling "why" to see the forest through the trees, so will your students.

- Why/How will your life improve from this?
- Why do you need to learn this?

- What are you gaining from this?
- What reward will you get, or punishment will you avoid?

Perhaps most important with teaching, it's not necessarily about the end point or achieving a goal. Sometimes, just to galvanize someone into giving an effort should be considered a success. It may be frustrating, but you are teaching for your student's benefit, so your impatience has no part in it. If you can give them positive feedback and move the goal posts so their effort is rewarded, they will feel more willing about their learning process.

Your Biggest Obstacle

I saved the biggest and best for last. Your biggest obstacle to learning will almost always be yourself and your sense of pride in one way or another. Consider someone who wants to learn to skate.

She wants to learn, but the skating rink is always full of people she knows from school. She doesn't want to fall in front of them. She has lessons, but doesn't venture outside her comfort zone because she doesn't want to feel embarrassed. She only ever does things she is completely certain she will succeed at. As you can imagine, this results in barely perceptible, incremental growth. She feels like her quest of learning to skate has

become pointless because she is not improving, and she quits and takes up golf.

What's the lesson here?

Her pride kept her from learning because she didn't want to look bad in front of other people. In fact, she abhorred the thought, and wouldn't even allow the thought of embarrassment to enter her mind. It kept her from learning.

We do similar things all the time, and they greatly hinder our ability to learn and accomplish as much as we truly can.

We are sometimes unable to admit when we are wrong, even if we know we are, because we don't want to *lose face* or be characterized as the loser in an interaction. We close our minds and ears to the correct path because we want to be seen as a smart winner.

We, like the skating student, sometimes feel the need to look good in front of others. We want to maintain an air of superiority, and are incapable of showing vulnerability for fear that we will be picked apart mercilessly. This is why many of us despise asking questions in front of others. We think we will be judged, and we would rather be wrong and not learn than lose the pretense of understanding and intelligence.

We sometimes refuse instruction altogether because

we don't want to be put in a lower position, so to speak, to someone else. We don't give them permission to show us, and we carry on doing things the wrong way simply because we don't want to feel wrong or dumb while being taught. We feel that needing help is a sign of weakness, and we want to do things ourselves to show our strength and confidence. Little do we realize that this is frequently what leads to overcompensating behavior, and it's extremely apparent to most bystanders that we are trying to cover something up.

We frequently make excuses for our own behavior or failures. Sometimes it's uncertain who we are trying to convince: ourselves or other people. We'll attribute our failures to other people or external circumstances, never holding ourselves accountable or seeing where the responsibility really lies. Better yet, we are smart enough to come up with *smart* excuses to rationalize behavior – excuses that other people will believe, and that you might even believe sometimes.

Finally, we are afraid of appearing like we don't have the answers, so we act like we have them all. We aren't open to alternative solutions because we feel like they invalidate our intelligence, which leads to glaring blind spots and knowledge gaps, because we ignore other perspectives. It's never okay to answer with "I don't know" because we feel like that denotes ignorance and stupidity. We desperately want to be seen a certain way, and those people always seem to have answers.

Of course, we don't realize that those people say "I don't know" more frequently than anyone to foster discussion and find the answers.

13

Albert Einstein's Logic Riddle

EINSTEIN WROTE the following riddle. He stated that 98% of the world could not solve it. This may not have been a riddle that was supposed to indicate intelligence, because others have implied that it just requires attention and patience:

There are five houses in five different colors in a row. In each house lives a person with a different nationality. The five owners drink a certain type of beverage, smoke a certain brand of cigar, and keep a certain pet. No owners have the same pet, smoke the same brand of cigar, or drink the same beverage.

Other facts:

1. The Brit lives in the red house.
2. The Swede keeps dogs as pets.
3. The Dane drinks tea.

4. The green house is on the immediate left of the white house.
5. The green house's owner drinks coffee.
6. The owner who smokes Pall Mall rears birds.
7. The owner of the yellow house smokes Dunhill.
8. The owner living in the center house drinks milk.
9. The Norwegian lives in the first house.
10. The owner who smokes Blends lives next to the one who keeps cats.
11. The owner who keeps the horse lives next to the one who smokes Dunhill.
12. The owner who smokes Bluemasters drinks beer.
13. The German smokes Prince.
14. The Norwegian lives next to the blue house.
15. The owner who smokes Blends lives next to the one who drinks water.

The question is: WHO OWNS THE FISH?

Skip ahead for the answer. .

.

.

.

.

.

.

.

.

.

.

.

.

.

.

.

The German sits in his Green House, smoking his Prince cigars, drinking coffee, and watching his FISH.

The rest goes like this:

1st House: Yellow, Norwegian, Water, Cats, Dunhill

2nd House: Blue, Dane, Tea, Horse, Blends

3rd House: Red, Brit, Milk, Birds, Pall Malls

4th House: Green, German, Coffee, FISH, Prince

5th House: White, Swede, Beer, Dogs, Bluemasters

Conclusion

What started with a misguided attempt at talking to Jessica from Spanish class has turned me into what some would call world class at learning and teaching – at least, that's what my clients tell me.

I hope you take these lessons and use them to learn better and cram more knowledge into your head than you ever thought before. What you have to remember is that it won't be easy at first, and it will feel like you are learning how to learn all over again, just like a toddler.

Soon though, you will realize that you are retaining far more than usual, reading faster, and becoming generally more knowledgeable, in seemingly less time. Your friends will ask you for your secrets at how you are achieving top grades while working less than them.

Your answer? Learning how to learn.

Best of luck,

Peter

Summary

Chapter 1. Shattering Myths

There are a few myths about learning that hold us back unintentionally, and keep us from our potential. Among them are thinking that failure is always bad, that our learning abilities are capped by our intelligence, and that more studying and exposure is always the better path.

Chapter 2. Foundations for Better Learning

As a precursor to improving your learning, you must be aware that multi-tasking is a complete myth, and learn techniques to focus yourself and pay attention to your own attention. You will see how you should generally approach and structure matters through the pyramid of learning and four levels of competence.

Chapter 3. Know and Understand Thyself

If you don't know yourself and what you prefer, you are forever operating through inefficiency. There are a few models of learning styles and preference, highlighted by the VARK and seven styles models.

Chapter 4. Faster and More Efficient Reading

Better reading is a matter of speed, efficiency, comprehension, and retention. You can train speed reading separately, while the other factors are a matter of analysis and active participation in reading rather than passive.

Chapter 5. The Art of Taking Great Notes

Taking better notes consists of four phases: taking, creating, analysis, and feedback. You can also use the Cornell Method of taking notes.

Chapter 6. Best Practices for Practicing

Deliberate practice is the key to truly growing expertise in something. Analyzing negative feedback and practicing at the edge of your abilities are close behind.

Chapter 7. Elephant Memory Techniques

Most people want information to make it to their long-term memory. Spaced repetition is the best method for memory retention, while flashcards, mnemonics, and constructing a story narrative with information also help.

Chapter 8. Make Learning Secondary

If you can set out to accomplish a goal that just so happens to require skill acquisition, this is the easiest way to learn – by making the learning secondary.

Chapter 9. How to CRAM

Cramming is the attempt to stuff as much information into the hazy area just short of your long-term memory, but beyond your short-term memory. Chunking, summarizing, and making analytical connections between concepts are your best bets.

Chapter 10. Learning by Science

Science can often reveal counterintuitive ways to learn better. Separate studies have shown that exercise boosts your brain power, changing locations helps memory retention, the Feynman Technique helps you learn what you don't know, and you can actually learn some things during sleep.

Chapter 11. Smart Goals

The best types of goals are S.M.A.R.T. – an acronym that stands for Specific, Measurable, Attainable, Relevant, Time-bound.

Chapter 12. The Trio

A final set of tips for learning come in the form of incubation, how to teach more effectively, and why your biggest obstacle to learning just might be your ego.

Chapter 13. Albert Einstein's Logic Riddle

No spoilers here!